STUDIES IN AMERICAN POPULAR HISTORY AND CULTURE

Edited by
JEROME NADELHAFT

A ROUTLEDGE SERIES

STUIES IN AMERICAN POPULAR HISTORY AND CULTURE

JEROME NADELHAFT, *General Editor*

DECONSTRUCTING POST–WWII NEW YORK CITY

The Literature, Art, Jazz, and Architecture of an Emerging Global Capital

Robert Bennett

Routledge
New York & London

Published in 2003 by
Routledge
29 West 35th Street
New York, NY 10001
www.routledge-ny.com

Published in Great Britain by
Routledge
11 New Fetter Lane
London EC4P 4EE
www.routledge.co.uk

Routledge is an imprint of the Taylor & Francis Group
Printed in the United States of America on acid-free paper.

10 9 8 7 6 5 4 3 2

Library of Congress Cataloging-in-Publication Data

Bennett, Robert.
    Deconstructing post–WWII New York City : the literature, art, jazz, and architec-
ture of an emerging global capital / by Robert Bennett.
        p. cm.
    Includes biblographical references and index.
    ISBN 0-415-94606-9
    1. New York (N.Y.)—Intellectual life—20th century. 2. New York (N.Y.)—Social
conditions—20th century. 3. New York (N.Y.)—Civilization—20th century.
4. Intellectuals—New York (State)—New York—History—20th century. 5. Arts and
society—New York (State)—New York—History—20th century. 6. Avant-garde
(Aesthetics)—New York (State)—New York—History—20th century. 7. Modernism
(Aesthetics)—New York (State)—New York—History—20th century. 8. City and
town life—New York (State)—New York—History—20th century. 9. Architecture—
Social aspects—New York (State)—New York—History—20th century 10. City planning—New York (State)—New York—History—20th century. I. Title: Deconstructing
post-World War II New York City. II. Title.
F128.52.B44 2003
700'.9747'109045—dc21   2003046996

To my family:
Chris, Theo, Sage, and Nina

"I am for an art that does something other than sit on its ass in a museum"
—Claes Oldenburg, from "I am For an Art"

Contents

Illustrations

Acknowledgments

While working on this project, I have been generously supported by many colleagues, friends, and family members. Enda Duffy, Giles Gunn, and Shirley Geok-Lin Lim, in particular, have provided me with both generous encouragement and insightful criticism. Without their mentoring and comments, this book would have been much less than it is. Other colleagues and friends who have helped inspire this project in ways both large and small, include Eliav Appelbaum, Michael Austin, Jacob Berman, Claire Goodman, John Inouye, Sumita Lall, Suzanne Lundquist, Aldon Nielsen, Michael Perry, Rita Raley, Garth St. Omer, Jace Turner, Kim Stone, and Rob Wallace. Without the on-going conversations that I have had with these fellow travelers, the intellectual scope and energy that I have brought to this work would have been significantly diminished.

Financially, this project has been generously supported by a Fletcher Jones Fellowship and an Interdisciplinary Humanities Center Predoctoral Fellowship from the University of California, Santa Barbara. Some of the initial research for this project was also completed while I was working as a research assistant for a United States Information Agency Summer Institute for the Study of American Literature organized by Shirley Geok-Lin Lim. This Institute not only provided me with financial support during the early stages of this project, but it also helped finance travel to New York City that helped me begin researching and developing this project. Part of chapter four was also presented at the Modern Language Association annual conference, and the audience and panel commentators offered insightful comments that have helped me to improve my arguments and analysis in this chapter.

I am also grateful to Taylor & Francis, Inc. for granting permission to reprint a revised version of my essay, " 'Literature as Destruction of Space': The Precarious Architecture of Barbara Guest's Spatial Imagination," in chapter four. This essay originally appeared in *Women's Studies: An Interdisciplinary Journal* 30.1 (2001), and it is copyrighted (2001) from *Women's Studies: An Interdisciplinary Journal* by Robert Bennett. It is reproduced by permission of Taylor & Francis, Inc., http://www.routledge-ny.com. New Directions Publishing Corporation has also granted permission to reprint a selection from "The Tourist Eye" by George Oppen, from *Collected Poems*, copyright ©1975 by George Oppen. I would also like to thank Culver Pictures, Esto Photographics, the Museum of the City of New York, and Mr. and Mrs. Earl McGrath for granting permission to reproduce several photographs and paintings.

Finally, I reserve my most sincere and complete gratitude for my family who has supported me in every way possible. My wife, Chris, has helped me work through both the intellectual and the personal issues involved in publishing a book while raising three children. She has given me time when I have needed to write, and she has helped me get away from writing when I have needed time for more important things. She has listened to and engaged my ideas, and she has thoughtfully commented on many early and barely comprehensible drafts of this project. She has both supported and distracted me in every way possible, and both this book and my life have benefited invaluably from her distractions as much as from her support.

Our children—Theo, Sage, and Nina—have provided less practical but equally important assistance. With their vibrant and evolving lives, they have been a constant, living reminder of the dangers of trying to contain human life within little boxes. They have shown me that life, like cities and art, is sometimes best left unplanned, wild, open, spontaneous, and free. On some days, they have hindered my exploration of the relationship between post-WWII literature and urban space. On other days, they have opened the conceptual windows through which I have come to understand it. As they grow older, I hope that I can return to them some of the insights that they have given me into the nature of cities, literature, and life.

DECONSTRUCTING POST–WW II NEW YORK CITY

Introduction

"Little Boxes Made of Ticky-Tacky . . . Little Boxes All the Same"

Deconstructing the Socio-Spatial Regime of Post-WWII New York City

Little boxes on the hillside / Little boxes made of ticky-tacky / Little boxes on the hillside / Little boxes all the same. / There's a pink one and a green one / And a blue one and a yellow one / And they're all made out of ticky-tacky / And they all look just the same.
—Malvina Reynolds, from "Little Boxes"

I love this hairy city.
It's wrinkled like a detective story
and noisy and getting fat and smudged
lids hood the sharp hard black eyes.
—Frank O'Hara, from "To the Mountains in New York"

A. A violent order is disorder; and
B. A great disorder is an order. These
Two things are one. (Pages of illustrations).
—Wallace Stevens, from "Connoisseur of Chaos"

DESCRIBING THE SUBURBS AS A SERIES OF "LITTLE BOXES" THAT ARE "ALL MADE OUT of ticky-tacky" and "all look just the same," Malvina Reynolds's folk song, "Little Boxes," criticizes the spatial restructuring of post-WWII American cities. Using the same repetitive, banal images to represent both suburban architecture's monotonous spatial aesthetics on the one hand, and suburban subjects' cultural homogeneity on the other, it demonstrates how architectural and urban spaces reflect the socio-political ideologies of the material cultures that produce them. Its recurring images of nearly identical, bland "little boxes made of ticky-tacky" associate suburban architecture with such "square" values as social conformity, emotional sobriety, cultural homogeneity, and political complacency. Its frequent oscillations between architectural and social themes depict suburban space as a kind of

3

psycho-spatial straightjacket that normalizes suburban subjects into a homogeneous community of isomorphic citizens who, like their homes, are also "all made out of ticky-tacky" and "all look just the same." By representing this interrelationship between spatial and social practices, "Little Boxes" demonstrates how suburban spaces helped shape post-WWII America's dominant cultural consensus: they were politically charged sites where the era's ideological tensions were symbolically inscribed, socially reproduced, and—as Reynolds's satire demonstrates—also politically contested.

While Reynolds's song specifically protests the suburbanization of post-WWII San Francisco, it describes a more extensive spatial paradigm that pervaded the post-WWII restructuring of both American cities in general and New York City in particular. Rejecting the neo-classical and Art Deco styles that had dominated New York architecture for the first half of the twentieth century, post-WWII architects and urban planners turned instead to more modern spatial practices, ranging from the clean lines of Bauhaus modernism and streamlined aesthetics of Raymond Hood's McGraw-Hill Building to the rational urban designs of Frank Lloyd Wright's Broadacre City and Le Corbusier's Radiant City. While these spatial practices were neither indigenous nor new to post-WWII New York City, that is where they were first synthesized into a comprehensive urban paradigm that dominated urban redevelopment at a "decisive moment when the waning Classicism of the nineteenth century gave way almost completely to the Modernism that had been making significant inroads in America since the early 1930s" (Stern et al., *New York 1960*, 9). Even though this shift in spatial sensibility was "typical of American architecture and urbanism as a whole," it was "nowhere more vividly realized than in New York, where the complete revision of the zoning ordinance virtually legislated not only Modernist urbanism but also Modernist aesthetics" (Stern et al., *New York 1960*, 9). With minimal deviation from this modernist spatial ideology, post-WWII New York City was radically reconstructed according to what Le Corbusier described as the "pure geometry" of "mathematical forms," "logical productions," "geometrical cells," "right angles," and the "straight line, inevitably; for the construction of buildings, sewers and tunnels, highways, pavements" (22, xxii, xxvi, 25, 10). Monotonous suburban architecture flourished in sprawling new developments such as William J. Levitt's Levittown.

Levittown, New York. Levitt & Sons. Aerial view showing the first 2,000 houses. 1947. (Reprinted by permission from Culver Pictures)

Similarly, Corinne Demas's memoir, *Eleven Stories High: Growing Up in Stuyvesant Town, 1948–1968*, describes how people were "bewildered" by the abstract spatial design of modernist urban housing projects where "everything was homogeneous, symmetrical, and orderly":

> In an episode that sounds like familiar fiction, but was in fact quite true, a father in my building went home by mistake to the identical building across the way. He went upstairs in the identical elevator, got off at his floor, went to his apartment, where the door was unlocked (this was the fifties: doors were unlocked during the day so the kids could run freely from one apartment to another) and walked in. He wondered if his wife had gotten new furniture, shouted "Hello!" to her, and a strange woman screamed in the bathroom. (5)

Manhattan's corporate architecture also conformed to a similar abstract spatial logic as architects replicated the geometrical aesthetics of Gordon Bunshaft's Lever House and Ludwig Mies van der Rohe's Seagram's Building in rows of nearly-identical, gridded glass-and-steel box skyscrapers. As Ezra Stoller's photograph of the homogeneous skyscrapers along Sixth Avenue brilliantly captures, International Style Modernist corporate architecture restructured Manhattan's central business districts with augmented variations on the repetitive, ersatz suburban architecture criticized by Malvina Reynolds. From Manhattan's urban core of International Style corporate skyscrapers and concrete-slab housing projects to the farthest reaches of the city's sprawling suburbs, architects and urban planners extended neo-Corbusian straight lines, right angles, and geometrical grids across the surface of post-WWII New York City.

Like Malvina Reynolds, however, many writers, artists, and intellectuals contested this spatial restructuring of their city. Using a paradoxical logic similar to Wallace Stevens's "Connoisseur of Chaos," they represented post-WWII New York urbanism as an "order" so "violent" that it produced more "disorder" than order (215). For example, Allen Ginsberg's "Howl" denounces the city's "Robot apartments," "invisible suburbs," and "sphinx[es] of cement and aluminum" not simply for the "pure machinery" of their homogeneous spatial aesthetics but also for the psycho-social damage that they inflict upon urban subjects by "bash[ing] open the skulls," eating "up the brains and imagination," and "destroy[ing]" the "best minds" of his generation (131, 126). Lawrence Ferlinghetti's *A Coney Island of the Mind* also criticizes postwar suburbanization for producing "freeways fifty lanes wide / on a concrete continent / spaced with

View of International Style Modernist skyscrapers along Sixth Avenue, New York City. From right to left, Exxon Building (Harrison, Abramovitz & Harris, 1971), McGraw-Hill Building (Harrison, Abramovitz & Harris, 1972), Celanese Building (Harrison, Abramovitz & Harris, 1973), and J. P. Stevens Tower (Emery Roth & Sons, 1971). Ezra Stoller © Esto. (Reprinted by permission from Esto Photographics)

bland billboards / illustrating imbecile illusions of happiness" (9). By depicting the "strange suburban shores" of this "kissproof world of plastic toiletseats tampax taxis" as producing only a limited "demi-democracy" of "strung-out citizens / in painted cars," it also demonstrates how suburbia's spatial homogeneity both reflects and helps produce a similar socio-political conformity (10–13). Similarly, Gilbert Sorrentino's *Steelwork*, a fragmented modernist depiction of the dissolution of a postwar working-class Italian American community in Brooklyn, concludes by describing a park "choked with bulldozers, cranes, heaps of rock and soil, where they were tearing out a gigantic strip of grass and trees to make a highway to connect with the new parkway going through along the bay, and then out the length of Long Island" (177). Even though Sorrentino also blames the community's dissolution on the war, American popular culture, and the community's own internal contradictions, he directs his parting shot against Robert Moses's highways, which imposed abstract concrete grids on top of urban communities with little concern for their organic socio-spatial topography. By concluding with this image, Sorrentino insinuates that urban communities not only fall apart because they internally self-destruct, but they are also torn apart by external attempts to "rationally" reorganize them. All three works represent post-WWII New York urbanism not simply as bland and homogeneous but more specifically as a "violent order" that disrupts the city's complex socio-spatial fabric.

Instead of "rationalizing" the city to conform to this "violent order," the post-WWII New York avant-garde developed new aesthetic strategies to express a more erratic, chaotic sense of urban space. Like Stevens's "Connoisseur of Chaos," which describes a "great disorder" as a kind of "order," they defended urban diversity by exploring more eccentric urban subjects, spaces, and cultures (215). In *Invisible Man*, Ralph Ellison depicts a complex urban subject who partially escapes the psycho-social violence of the racially segregated and bureaucratic city by becoming "invisible" and going into "hibernation" in a subterranean jazz cave that he discovers "in a building rented strictly to whites, in a section of the basement that was shut off and forgotten during the nineteenth century" (5–6). Violating the unities of both time and space, this eccentric "hole in the ground" exists on an alternative spatio-temporal plane in a "border area" of Harlem with a "slightly different sense of time, you're never quite on the beat. Sometimes you're ahead and sometimes behind. Instead of the swift and imperceptible flowing of time, you are aware of its nodes, those points where time stands still or from which it leaps ahead" (5–6, 8). Frank O'Hara's poetry also contests the geometrical restructuring of post-WWII New York City by mapping the erratic topographies of his "lunch hour" walks among the city's "hum-colored cabs" and past the "languorously agitating" Negroes and "blond chorus girl[s]" in Times Square where

"Everything / suddenly honks" before he stops for a "cheeseburger at JULI-
ET'S CORNER" (*Collected Poems*, 257–8). Representing and magnifying
the unique quiddity of the diverse spaces that he passes through, O'Hara's
"lunch hour" poems explore what the city can be like—and in fact what it
is like—for urban subjects who are not confined, either spatially or psychologically, by the city's homogeneous spatial grid. In other poems,
O'Hara explicitly challenges the functionalist pretensions of International
Style Modernist architecture by imagining dysfunctional, ludic spaces
where he can drop a "hot dog" into "one of the Seagram Building's / foun-
tains" (*Collected Poems*, 476). Turning away from the city of Moloch with
its "skyscrapers stand[ing] in the long streets like endless Jehovahs,"
Ginsberg's "Howl" also explores such counter-hegemonic urban spaces as
the "negro streets at dawn," "tenement roofs illuminated" by
"Mohammedan angels," and endless subway rides "from Battery to holy
Bronx on benzedrine" (131, 126). In "My Sad Self," Ginsberg rambles
through "all these streets leading / so crosswise, honking, lengthily, / by
avenues," but he is also aware of how these streets are constantly "stalked
by high buildings" (202). All of these works represent complex, heterogeneous urban spaces and subjects, but not simply as expressions of the city's
chaotic urban diversity. Instead, they self-consciously attempt to document,
defend, or produce eccentric urban experiences that exist beneath the surface, on the margins, or along the interstices of the city's more homogeneous urban center. They explore aberrant spatio-temporal dimensions,
heterogeneous urban topographies, and deviant urban paradigms, but they
explicitly associate these anomalous urban spaces with some kind of alternative, counter-hegemonic city-within-the-city or some marginalized urban
space that is dominated, opposed, stalked, haunted, or repressed by the
corporate city that surrounds it.

THE CITY AND THE ARTS: THEORIZING URBAN SPACE AND URBAN CULTURE

While previous analyses of New York culture—from Peter Conrad's *The
Art of the City* (1984) and William Sharpe and Leonard Wallock's *New
York: Cultural Capital of the World, 1940–1965* (1988) to Phillip Lopate's
Writing New York: A Literary Anthology (1998) and William B. Scott and
Peter M. Rutkoff's *New York Modern: The Arts and the City* (1999)—have
interpreted the city's dynamic modern culture as an expression of its com-
plex urban environment, critics generally describe both the city itself and
cultural representations of it as simply sharing a common chaotic form.
Consequently, they tend to reduce post-WWII New York culture to a
mechanical, isomorphic reflection of its material context. For example,
Phillip Lopate argues that New York writing:

flows from the rhythm and mode of being that this singular place imposes on everyone who lives in or even visits it at length. New York's essence, literary or otherwise, grows out of the street experience, the basis for an aesthetic of a ragged, miraculous simultaneity. . . . its man-made geography and network of mass transports provide the basic cue, the beat from which all else follows. (xvii)

Scott and Rutkoff also contend that the "subject of New York Modern remained urban life, in all its elusive complexity and variety," and Wallock argues that the "experience of life in New York—its intensity, dynamism, and complexity—was the driving force behind the artistic innovations of the 1940s and 1950s" (Scott and Rutkoff xvii; Wallock 11). While it is indisputable that New York City's complex urban environment has significantly influenced the city's culture, that urban environment cannot be reduced solely to "intensity, dynamism, and complexity" any more than it can be simplistically identified as the "driving force behind the artistic innovations of the 1940s and 1950s" (Wallock 11). On the contrary, architects and urban planners radically reconstructed post-WWII New York City using spatial practices that were deliberately designed to homogenize, organize, and police the city's complex heterogeneity. If post-WWII New York culture is to be interpreted as critically engaging its urban material context, then the socio-spatial topography of that context, with its various lines of demarcation and competing public cultures, needs to be more carefully mapped. In addition, post-WWII New York culture needs to be fundamentally reconceptualized not as a mechanical reflection of its chaotic urban environment but rather as a political and imaginative defense of the city's urban heterogeneity against the neo-Corbusian straightjackets of post-WWII urbanism's brave new cities of "little boxes made of ticky-tacky . . . little boxes all the same." Instead of promoting a naïve urban primitivism that uncritically equates urban spaces with exotic notions of diversity and chaos, post-WWII New York literature develops a critical awareness that cities are socio-spatial battle grounds where diverse social and spatial practices clash—some homogeneous and others heterogeneous, some centripetal and others centrifugal, some backed by the economic and political power of corporate capital and others emerging out of the contradictions and along the margins of the capitalist political economy.

Deconstructing Post-WWII New York City is an interdisciplinary analysis of this confrontation between architects and urban planners' homogeneous reconstruction of post-WWII New York City on the one hand, and the post-WWII New York avant-garde's exploration of more heterogeneous urban spaces on the other. Situating post-WWII New York literature within the material context of American urban history, it analyzes how literary movements such as the Beat Generation, the New York School of poetry, and the Black Arts Movement develop a materially located and politically engaged critical urban discourse. In particular, it argues that this urban discourse profoundly influences not only the content but also the aesthetic form of post-WWII New York literature. Post-WWII New York writers did create new aesthetic strategies to critique the geometrical restructuring of their city, but they also saw strong parallels between their exploration of alternative urban spaces and the new experimental aesthetic practices that they wanted to develop. The principal objective of my project, therefore, is not simply to describe how the post-WWII New York avant-garde critiques the homogeneous spatial geometry of modernist architecture and urban planning, but rather to explain the specific role that the aesthetic imagination plays in the formulation of this urban critique. The conflict between International Style Modernism's and the cultural avant-garde's different conceptions of urban space does demarcate a crucial site of social and political conflict that reflects the ideological tensions of post-WWII American culture, but there is also an aesthetic dimension to this conflict that significantly influenced the avant-garde's reconceptualization of aesthetic practices. After all, why did the New York avant-garde begin critiquing post-WWII urbanism in aesthetic works produced as early as the late 1940s, more than a decade before similar arguments became popular among urban and architectural theorists with the publication of Kevin Lynch's *The Image of the City* (1960), Jane Jacobs's *The Death and Life of Great American Cities* (1961), and Robert Venturi's *Complexity and Contradiction in Architecture* (1966)? Was there some enabling condition that made it easier to express this critique in aesthetic texts than in architectural theories and urban manifestos? Moreover, why did post-WWII writers, artists, and other cultural producers explore alternative urban spaces so passionately in their art but—with a few exceptions such as Norman Mailer—never take a particularly active role in politically advocating the actual production of these spaces in the real, material city? Did they see aesthetic experimentation as the front line in a larger battle that would eventually influence public attitudes and urban politics, or were they simply more interested in artistic cities of the mind than in material cities of concrete, glass, and steel? And why did so many members of the post-WWII New York avant-garde, working both in and between a wide range of artistic media, explicitly connect their exploration of alternative urban spaces with their attempt to develop new experimental aesthetic practices? By connecting the New York avant-garde's urban critique to these kinds of aesthetic issues, *Deconstructing Post-WWII New York City* explores various "architextural" relationships between writers' representations of architectural and urban spaces and their experimentation with new aesthetic textual structures.

This conflict between post-WWII New York architects' and artists' different conceptions of urban space largely derives from the trans-Atlantic translation of European modernism to New York City. Beginning with the

Armory Show in 1913, European modernism exerted a powerful influence on New York culture as the city's artists, writers, and other cultural producers increasingly imitated European modernism's complex, fragmented aesthetic practices. The Museum of Modern Art, in particular, played a prominent role in promoting European modernism. Trapped within what Tom Wolfe described as a "colonial complex inflated to prodigious dimensions," the museum ensured that "European modernism in painting and sculpture was established, *institutionalized*, overnight, in the most overwhelming way, as the standard for the arts in America. The International Style exhibition was designed to do the same thing for European modernism in architecture" (38–9). As Wolfe explains, Henry-Russell Hitchcock and Philip Johnson's catalogue for the International Style exhibit passionately advocated European avant-garde architecture as "nothing less than the first great universal style since the Medieval and Classical revivals, and the first truly modern style since the Renaissance" (Wolfe 38). This advocacy of International Style Modernism was reinforced by the exigencies of WWII, which forced several European architects to immigrate to the United States. Receiving appointments at prestigious institutions such as Harvard and the Illinois Institute of Technology, Walter Gropius, Mies van der Rohe, and other European architects quickly established the International Style as the dominant paradigm of post-WWII American architecture and urban planning. As a result of these trans-Atlantic exchanges, post-WWII New York culture largely reproduced European modernism's opposition between the "pure geometry" of modernist architecture and the fragmented aesthetic strategies promoted by modernist artists and writers. Consequently, the post-WWII New York avant-garde's exploration of alternative urban paradigms was not only significantly influenced by the aesthetic practices of European modernism, in addition to the city's complex urban environment, but it also developed in opposition to, rather than as an isomorphic reflection of, the dominant spatial paradigm of post-WWII New York urbanism.

This opposition between the spatial and aesthetic practices of European modernism was further intensified as these practices were adapted to the new material context of post-WWII New York City. As a result of Europe's declining and the United States' rising geopolitical power, New York City emerged as the de facto economic and cultural capital of the post-WWII world. New York architects, artists, writers, and other intellectuals responded to this shifting geopolitical topography by developing new cultural practices that would express the city's increasing international power and authority. One of the clearest barometers of this change can be seen in the series of articles that Clement Greenberg published in *The Partisan Review* during 1948. In these regular installments of art criticism, Greenberg plotted modern art's relocation from Paris to New York City as the "main premises of Western art . . . migrated to the United States, along with the center of gravity of industrial production and political power" ("The Decline of Cubism," 483). In particular, Greenberg argued that the New York School of abstract expressionism epitomized an "important new phase in the history of painting" that extended the fragmented aesthetics of European modernism into even more arbitrary, chaotic, and self-reflexive aesthetic practices. Expressing a "deep-seated . . . contemporary sensibility," this proto-postmodern extension of modernist aesthetics explored how "hierarchical distinctions have been exhausted, that no area or order of experience is either intrinsically or relatively superior to any other" ("The Crisis of the Easel Picture," 484). Extending the architectural and urban theories of the European avant-garde in the opposite direction, architects and urban planners reconstructed post-WWII New York City according to an increasingly geometrical spatial ideology. They adapted International Style Modernist architecture to "serve the purposes of expedient commercialism" by promoting an aesthetic style of "singular, obsessive minimalism," thereby retaining the International Style's goal of transforming "all aesthetic and functional requirements into pure geometry" while jettisoning its "high social, urban and technological ideals" (Stern et al., *New York 1960*, 47). By extending the spatial and cultural practices of European modernism in opposite directions, post-WWII New York culture drove an even deeper wedge between European modernism's already antagonistic spatial and artistic practices.

In addition, this opposition between post-WWII New York architects' and artists' different conceptions of urban space was further exacerbated by each group's different relationship to the political economy of post-WWII corporate capitalism. Because architectural and urban projects require such extensive financial resources, spatial practices tend to conform more closely to the socio-political ideologies of the material cultures that produce them. As Fredric Jameson explains, of "all the arts, architecture is the closest constitutively to the economic, with which, in the form of commissions and land values, it has a virtually unmediated relationship" (5). Less overdetermined by these economic constraints, artists and writers have more relative autonomy to develop a critical stance against the reigning political ideologies of their day. Without either reducing architecture to mere ideology or inflating art and literature into some kind of transcendental cultural critique, these disciplines' different relationships to the capitalist political economy give them different degrees of cultural autonomy. In post-WWII New York City, these different degrees of autonomy helped expand the divide between architects and urban planners, who frequently advocated spatial practices that expressed the ideology of corporate capitalism, and artists and writers, who attempted to create new aesthetic practices that would challenge those corporate ideologies. As the spatial restructuring of post-WWII New York City edged ever closer to a brutal expression of corporate ideologies, the cultural avant-garde used the relative autonomy of its art to challenge both this spatial restructuring and the corporate ideologies that it reflected. While the boundary line between these competing corporate and anti-corporate ideologies was neither impermeable nor irreversible, it did help establish a general framework for the conflicting tensions within post-WWII New York culture.

The conflict between post-WWII New York architects' and artists' different conceptions of urban space reflected not only the trans-Atlantic translation of European modernism and post-WWII New York culture's extension of European precedents, but it was also shaped by the different relationships that spatial and aesthetic practices have to the capitalist political economy. By positing an isomorphic correspondence between the urban space and urban culture of post-WWII New York City, however, previous critics have generally ignored how these conditions enabled the cultural avant-garde to develop a critical urban discourse that not only represented but also critically analyzed and imagined alternatives to the city's spatial restructuring. Overemphasizing how aesthetic practices reflect material contexts, critics have not sufficiently explained how the avant-garde's critical urban discourse also functioned as a deconstructive reading of urban space. The avant-garde did explore diverse, chaotic urban spaces, but it recognized that those spaces were situated against a larger, more powerful, and violently ordered corporate city that constantly threatened to destroy them. It read the city's socio-spatial geography as a complex ideological text whose lexicon and syntax were saturated with deeper cultural and political meanings, but it attempted to read that text deconstructively against the grain. It sought to destabilize the city's traditional architectural and urban centers by exploring various ambivalences—contradictions, discontinuities, contingencies, and marginal and interstitial regions—within the city's socio-spatial geography. As any deconstructive performance, this critical urban discourse remained partially caught within the same socio-spatial structures that it sought to deconstruct, but it also struggled to open up new possibilities for play within those structures. Like the heterogeneous urban spaces that it advocated, it produced a cultural critique that was more contingent than transcendent, more dynamic than static, more pragmatic than ideological, and more performative than definitive. By reducing urban culture to a more-or-less mechanical reflection of its material context, however, critics have largely obscured the role that the aesthetic imagination played in developing this urban critique, and they have fundamentally misconstrued the relationship between post-WWII New York City's urban space and urban culture, describing this relationship as imitative and complementary rather than agonistic and critical.

FRONTIERS FOR A FREE POETIC LIFE: THE AESTHETIC POLITICS OF URBAN SPACE

In addition to developing a critical urban discourse, the post-WWII New York avant-garde also considered its exploration of alternative urban spaces as a perfect metaphor for the new experimental aesthetic practices that it wanted to create. Many of the members of the post-WWII New York avant-garde not only critically analyzed the socio-political significance of urban space, but they did so in a decisively aesthetic manner. For example, Ferlinghetti's "Poetry and City Culture" identifies a strong correlation between the socio-spatial geography of cities and a "free poetic life." Because cities function as "a poetic center, a frontier for free poetic life," when "all the forces of our military-industrial perplex" transform cities into "one-dimensional" and "corporate" cities, this socio-spatial restructuring simultaneously endangers the "poetic life of the City, our subjective life, the subjective life of the individual." Critical of how the "soul / has gone out / of our cities / out of our buildings / out of the streets," Ferlinghetti's poem, "Modern Poetry is Prose," looks for a solution to this urban crisis not only in new urban paradigms but also in a revitalized aesthetic imagination, in the "still insurgent voice / lost among machines and insane nationalisms / still longing to break out" (8–9). In *A Coney Island of the Mind*, Ferlinghetti criticizes the "surrealist landscape" of post-WWII America's "supermarket suburbs," but he also waits "perpetually and forever / [for] a renaissance of wonder" that might enable the "discovery / of a new symbolic western frontier" (13, 53, 49). It is precisely this attempt to produce a "rebirth of wonder" and discover some "new symbolic western frontier" that energizes so much of the post-WWII New York avant-garde's exploration of urban space. Many writers, artists, and intellectuals defended various kinds of complex heterogeneous urban spaces, spaces that were threatened by the city's spatial restructuring, but they often defended these spaces for both aesthetic and political reasons. They saw these spaces as frontiers for developing new kinds of aesthetic practices because they materially embodied a different cultural and political logic than the corporate city that surrounded them.

Consequently, many post-WWII New York writers explored various kinds of "architextural" interrelationships between the spatial structure of architectural and urban spaces and the textual structure of narrative and poetic forms. Perhaps the clearest example of this can be found in the first two sections of Ginsberg's "Howl," which contrast two competing urban paradigms. The first section describes various counter-hegemonic urban spaces where "angelheaded hipsters" float "across the tops of cities contemplating jazz" and lounge "hungry and lonesome through Houston seeking jazz or sex or soup," while the second section describes the city's dominant urban paradigm of "invisible suburbs," "robot apartments," and "skyscrapers stand[ing] in the streets like endless Jehovahs" (126–7, 131). In addition, "Howl" also develops an "architextural" relationship between these competing urban paradigms and the contrasting aesthetic forms that he uses to represent them. Mirroring the homogeneous geometry of post-WWII American urbanism, the poem's second section creates a geometrical textual grid by dividing its lines into relatively uniform, short, choppy phrases that usually begin with the word "Moloch" and/or end with exclamation points. This produces a textual structure in which each phrase functions as a roughly equivalent linguistic cell within a larger textual grid. This grid-like structure is exemplified by the line: "Moloch! Moloch! Robot apartments! invisible suburbs! skeleton treasuries! blind capitals! demonic industries! spectral nations! invincible mad houses! granite cocks! monstrous bombs!" (131–2). With the exception of the repetition, "Moloch! Moloch!," and the three-word phrase "invincible mad houses," each phrase is a repetitive, two-word, adjective-noun exclamation within a larger textual structure that organizes them into identical rows of uniform images. Like the spatial grid imposed upon the urban space of post-WWII New York City, this textual grid homogenizes each element that it describes, depicting the city's "invisible suburbs," "robot apartments," and "granite cocks" as more-or-less equivalent elements subordinated within a homogeneous grid of isotropic images (131). It creates rows of identical little phrases made of ticky-tacky, little phrases all the same. In addition, "Howl" uses this textual grid to connect the spatial restructuring of post-WWII New York City to a wide range of social and political forces that this restructuring reflects: the "skeleton treasuries" of post-WWII corporate capitalism, the "monstrous bombs" of cold-war America, and the "invincible mad houses" that enforce conformity to "square" America's cultural norms and political ideologies (131–2). By placing all of these images within uniform linguistic cells connected by a homogeneous textual grid, "Howl" represents the strong interrelationship between the political economy of post-WWII corporate capitalism, the socio-spatial restructuring of post-WWII American cities, and the cultural politics of aesthetic forms.

Similarly, the first section of "Howl" also develops an "architextural" relationship between the alternative urban spaces that it describes and the experimental aesthetic strategies that it uses to describe them. At first glance, this section seems to develop the same kind of homogeneous textual grid that we find in the second section, with the individual cells demarcated by the repetition of the word "who." However, the disparate and excessive length of these lines, coupled with the heterogeneous, rambling, and eccentric images that fill them, produces an altogether different kind of textual structure. Instead of homogenizing each phrase to fit within a geometrical grid of isotropic linguistic cells, this section emphasizes the unique quiddity of each image by allowing it to occupy its own eccentric, irregular textual space, as exemplified by the line:

> Who dreamt and made incarnate gaps in Time & Space through images juxtaposed, and trapped the archangel of the soul between 2 visual images and joined the elemental verbs and set the noun and dash of consciousness together jumping with sensation of Pater Omnipotens Aeterna Deus. (130)

Mirroring the heterogeneous urban spaces that this section describes, its erratic lines do not conform to any uniform textual grid but instead proliferate in a profusion of disparate, ambiguous, discontinuous, and chaotic linguistic phrases. As the poem itself explains, this chaotic textual structure attempts to make "incarnate gaps" in the city's homogeneous spatial grid instead of imposing that abstract grid onto the city's complex heterogeneity. By exploring this "architextural" interrelationship between the spatial structures of counter-hegemonic urban regions and the textual structures of experimental poetry, "Howl" connects its critical analysis of urban space with its attempt to develop new aesthetic forms. It attempts to escape the city of Moloch by venturing into the "negro streets at dawn," but it does so largely to "recreate the syntax and measure of poor human prose," to explore the "rhythm and thought in his naked and endless head," and to join the "elemental verbs and set the noun and dash of consciousness together" (126, 130–1). It runs "through the icy streets," but it does so "obsessed with a sudden flash of the alchemy of the use of the ellipse the catalog the meter & the vibrating plane" (130). It challenges post-WWII America's brave new cities, but it does so by sounding "an eli eli lamma lamma sabacthoni saxophone cry that shivered the cities down to the last radio" (130). As much as any work in the canon of post-WWII American literature, it insists that the stakes involved in the post-WWII restructuring of American cities are as much aesthetic as they are political because there is a deep and intimate "architextural" connection between the spatial structure of cities and the aesthetic structure of cultural texts.

As these examples illustrate, many members of post-WWII New York avant-garde considered the aesthetic imagination as an integral component of their critical urban discourse. They made strong and repeated associations between their critique of post-WWII American urbanism, their exploration of alternative urban spaces, and their own experimental aesthetic practices. But why did they explore so many "architextural" interrelationships between cities and art, and what kind of cultural work was performed by these "architextural" comparisons? Why did they so strongly identify their new aesthetic experiments with alternative urban spaces? Why did Ginsberg locate his New American Poetry "under the El," in the "supernatural darkness of cold-water flats floating across the tops of cities," and in the "ghostly haze of Chinatown" (126, 129)? Why did

O'Hara's "6th Avenue conscience" focus its artistic vision on the "crimson welt of Number 16 East 11th," the "early morning passing Madison Avenue," or "12:20 in New York a Friday" (*Collected Poems*, 324–26)? What artistic inspiration did John Clellon Holmes find in the Beat Generation's subterranean city of "dingy backstairs 'pads,' Times Square cafeterias, bebop joints, night-long wanderings, meetings on street corners, hitchhiking, a myriad of 'hip' bars all over the city, and the streets themselves" (36)? Why did so many post-WWII New York writers turn to specific addresses in Times Square, Greenwich Village, and Harlem to find their aesthetic muses? Or conversely, why was their critical urban discourse so pervasively and tenaciously aesthetic? What role did "perpetually awaiting / a rebirth of wonder" and "recreat[ing] the syntax and measure of poor human prose" play in their socio-spatial analysis of the urban topography of post-WWII New York City (Ferlinghetti, *A Coney Island of the Mind*, 49; Ginsberg 130)? Why did they locate their critical urban discourse at some "architextural" corner where Washington Square, 42nd Street, and Lenox Avenue ran into the aesthetic imagination? In short, why did Ginsberg's poetry "walk down the streets of New York in the black cloak of French poetry," why did Tom Postell declare that "Gertrude Stein is long dead but under cover rides the torn down El," and why did Ferlinghetti's intertextual reading of Yeats not "think / of Arcady / and of its woods," but focus "instead / [on] all the gone faces / getting off at midtown places / with their hats and their jobs" as they rode the "Thirdavenue El" (Ginsberg 181; Postell, quoted in Nielsen, 83; Ferlinghetti 90–91)? What is going on in these repeated "architextural" juxtapositions of particular kinds of urban spaces with new modes of aesthetic experimentation?

I argue that there are several reasons why so many members of the post-WWII New York avant-garde explicitly connected their critical urban discourse with their experimental aesthetic practices. To begin with, many writers and artists aestheticized their urban critique because they came to see the material city itself as an aesthetic, semiotic construct. Like Rem Koolhaas's *Delirious New York*, which describes Manhattan as "the 20th century's Rosetta Stone," they "read" New York City's architectural and urban spaces as a kind of language or semiotic code that inscribed the ideological conflicts of the culture that produced them (9). In this sense, they "interpreted" the city as a politically charged work of art or a species of ideologically laden poetry written in glass, steel, and concrete on texts twenty blocks wide and fifty stories high. Consequently, they showed little concern for demarcating clear boundaries between the city and the arts because—as an aesthetic, semiotic construct—the city itself could be read, interpreted, and signified upon even by writers and artists who were unable to alter its physical topography.

Moreover, given New York City's axiological significance as the new cultural and economic "center" of the post-WWII world—as the de facto international capital of capital—the city's postwar restructuring reflected more than local political interests and stylish trends in architectural taste. It also materially inscribed the cultural logic of larger transformations occurring within the regional, national, and international structures of the capitalist political economy. This helps explain why the post-WWII New York avant-garde invested such passion in its representations of architectural and urban spaces—even if it did not politically agitate for specific urban reforms. Interpreting these spaces as symbolic expressions of larger national and international issues, the cultural avant-garde frequently used artistic representations of architectural and urban spaces as tropes for representing and analyzing a wide range of cultural, political, and philosophical concerns. Ferlinghetti and Ellison explored the city as a microcosm of American democracy, while Ginsberg and Ted Joans represented it as a brutal expression of the capitalist political economy, and Askia Muhammad Touré and Amiri Baraka analyzed it as a lucid articulation of racial conflicts. While these writers were also concerned about urban issues themselves, their critical analysis of urban spaces simultaneously functioned as a metaphorical trope for representing and analyzing the larger economic, political, and cultural forces that shaped the city's socio-spatial topography. Once again, this further blurred the boundary between urban and aesthetic concerns because writers frequently invoked the city as an aesthetic metaphor at the same time that they explored it as a thematic subject.

In addition to aestheticizing the city—both by seeing it as a cultural text itself and by using it as a metaphorical trope—the post-WWII New York avant-garde also turned to marginal, chaotic urban spaces as either an inspirational muse or a metaphor for its new aesthetic experimentation. Rejecting the Eliot-esque formalism that had come to dominate American poetry by the early 1950s, post-WWII New York writers wanted to explore more dynamic and chaotic aesthetic practices, and they saw complex, heterogeneous urban spaces as a perfect model for their new aesthetic ideal. Even in an early poem like "A Pathetic Note" (1951), O'Hara already established the rhythm of a particular urban space as the aesthetic standard by which he judged his poetic practice. Asking a friend to "[k]eep photographing the instant" when you "go down West / Fourteenth Street," O'Hara explains that this way "I will know what / it is like there," and "I will know you are at least all right" even if "my eyes seem incapable of the images I'd / hoped" (*Poems Retrieved*, 12). As O'Hara's admonition to "[k]eep photographing the instant" demonstrates, one of his primary aesthetic goals was to faithfully reproduce the existential topography of urban experiences. In early poems such as "Second Avenue," "Meditations in an Emergency," and "To the Mountains in New York," O'Hara laid the seeds for this urban aesthetic based on New York City's socio-spatial geography, and these seeds later blossomed into the more mature urban aesthetics of O'Hara's "I do this, I do that" and "lunch hour" poems. One can trace a clear line of development that extends from the "instant" photographed on "West / Fourteenth Street" in "A Pathetic Note" to the way that "The Day Lady Died" connects "12:20 in New York a Friday" to "I am sweating a lot by now and thinking of / leaning on the john door in the 5 SPOT / while she whispered along the keyboard / to Mal Waldron and everyone and I stopped breathing" (*Poems Retrieved*, 12; *Collected Poems*, 325). While an incidental poem like "A Pathetic Note" does not fully develop West Fourteenth Street's potential as an aesthetic model, the intricate "architextural" structure of "The Day Lady Died" demonstrates as profoundly as any urban poem how the socio-spatial quiddity of urban experience is pregnant with breath-taking aesthetic possibilities.

Invoking another urban metaphor, albeit a diametrically opposed one, Delmore Schwarz described the "present state of poetry" in the early 1950s as:

> a peaceful public park on a pleasant summer Sunday afternoon, so that if the majority of new poets write in a style and idiom which takes as its starting point the poetic idiom and literary taste of the generation of Pound and Eliot, the motives and attitudes at the heart of the writing possess an assurance which sometimes makes their work seem tame and sedate. (44)

Extending Schwarz's spatial metaphor still further, James E. B. Breslin has argued:

> If American poetry in the middle fifties resembled a peaceful public park on a pleasant summer Sunday afternoon, and if by the early sixties it had been transformed into a war zone, the air heavy with manifestos, then by the early 1980s the atmosphere has lightened and the scene more resembles a small affluent town in Northern California. (250)

As both these poems and critical comments demonstrate, different kinds of spaces provide appropriate analogies for different periods in post-WWII American poetry. On an aesthetic level, what the post-WWII New York avant-garde wanted to attack with its new aesthetic experiments was the "tame and sedate" aesthetic ideal of a "peaceful public park on a pleasant summer Sunday afternoon." Consequently, it developed its critical urban discourse, at least in part, because it believed that certain kinds of urban spaces either resembled or enabled the particular kinds of experimental aesthetics that it sought to create. It seems reasonable to conclude, therefore, that some of the avant-garde's highly aestheticized passion for complex heterogeneous urban spaces reflected either a redirected residual manifestation of or an analogical extension of its aesthetic quarrel with its artistic predecessors, and vice versa. In this sense, the avant-garde's critical urban discourse often functioned as a covert discussion of aesthetic form. It deliberately intermingled urban and aesthetic issues because it considered them complementary expressions of a similar cultural logic, and consequently its passionate urban discourse was frequently inseparable from the aesthetic battles that it waged against the preceding generation of American writers. The "skyscrapers stand[ing] in the long streets like endless Jehovahs" that Ginsberg attacks in "Howl" can be read almost interchangeably either as literal architectural structures or as metaphorical surrogates for the aesthetic structures developed by the preceding generation of American poets (131). There is a common "architextural" logic that connects the poem's exploration of urban spaces with its attempt to "recreate the syntax and measure of poor human prose" (130). In almost every image in the poem, one can sense this simultaneous "architextural" probing of the interrelationship between urban and aesthetic structures.

Another aesthetic dimension of the post-WWII New York avant-garde's critical urban discourse can be found in its interdisciplinary turn toward interart aesthetic experimentation. As several critics have noted, post-WWII New York writers and artists explored the aesthetic possibilities of urban space across many "styles and mediums" (Scott and Rutkoff xvii). Just as O'Hara produced "literary snapshots of New York" that recorded his "seemingly spontaneous observations while taking midday strolls" through midtown Manhattan, abstract expressionist visual artists such as Jackson Pollock "embraced the chaotic structures, random encounters, violent contrasts, and limitless possibilities of this most modern of cities;" iconoclastic musicians like John Cage "included chance occurrences, freeform experimentation, and chromatic dissonance—each one evocative of the modern urban environment;" and modern choreographers such as Merce Cunningham created works that "reverberated with the sights sounds, motion, and energy of the metropolis" (Wallock 11–14). Many members of the avant-garde either crossed over into multiple artistic media or experimented with new hybrid interart aesthetic practices, and many of these interart projects focused specifically on the urban space of post-WWII New York City. For example, Beat Generation and Black Arts writers such as Holmes, Kerouac, Baraka, and Jayne Cortez not only produced new literary forms modeled after jazz, but they also collaborated with musicians on jazz poetry performances, and they frequently connected their exploration of jazz aesthetics with their critical analysis of urban space. They saw bebop and post-bop jazz as a metaphor for the alternative urban spaces and aesthetic practices that they sought to promote. Similarly, New York School poets such as O'Hara, Barbara Guest, John Ashbery, and Kenneth Koch not only experimented with aesthetic strategies modeled after the visual arts and collaborated with visual artists on textual-visual interart projects, but they also explored how these interart aesthetic practices could be used both to represent and to analyze the city's complex socio-spatial topography.

At times, this interdisciplinary boundary crossing produced intricate webs of multiple interart influences. Joans and Ferlinghetti were not only both poets and painters, but they also collaborated with jazz musicians. Larry Rivers was a visual artist and a saxophonist who collaborated with several poets on various interart experiments, and James Breslin argues that O'Hara's numerous interart influences "proliferate maddeningly":

> he was familiar with and affected by film, dance, music, Russian writing (especially Pasternak and Mayakovsky), French poetry (especially dada and surrealism), American poetry (especially Whitman and Williams), and his taste in all media was open-minded and eclectic. O'Hara illustrates a receptivity to, rather than an anxiety about, a variety of influences, literary and otherwise. (212–3)

Yet, at the same time, one of the threads that helped congeal these numerous influences into some partially stable form was O'Hara's manic exploration of New York City. Consequently, O'Hara's work represents a quintessential distillation of the "architextural" tension that pervaded much of the post-WWII New York avant-garde. At the same time that writers, artists, musicians, and other cultural producers were working both in and across a wide range of different artistic media, they often shared a common goal of developing new aesthetic practices that critically engaged the city's socio-spatial topography. While this shared objective helped focus a wide range of aesthetic practices into a collective critical urban discourse, the broad interdisciplinary nature of that discourse further aestheticized it. The city helped congeal the post-WWII New York avant-garde's diverse practices into a coherent aesthetic project because it provided a common focus that many writers and artists shared, even though writers and artists analyzed the city through a wide range of heterogeneous aesthetic traditions. It is precisely this combination of a centrifugal passion for extensive interart aesthetic experimentation, combined with a centripetal interest in post-WWII New York City—both as a complex urban space and as a metaphor for developing new aesthetic practices—that so powerfully shaped the historical evolution of the New York avant-garde. On the one hand, writers and artists kept exploring farther and farther into the aesthetic ether of ever-more complex interart experiments, but at the same time they also kept returning to their concrete, existential experiences of the city. Continually oscillating between these two aesthetic and urban poles, the post-WWII New York avant-garde both developed new aesthetic practices that fundamentally reconfigured the disciplinary boundaries between different artistic media, and it also used those interart aesthetic practices to represent, analyze, and imagine alternatives to the socio-spatial restructuring of post-WWII New York City.

Focusing specifically on these kinds of aesthetic issues *Deconstructing Post-WWII New York City* analyzes the historical development of this conflict between the architects and urban planners who reconstructed post-WWII New York City and the writers, artists, and intellectuals who opposed this restructuring. Excavating the early history of this conflict, chapter 1 analyzes how the 1939–40 New York World's Fair provided one of the first major forums where the spatial practices that came to dominate post-WWII New York urbanism were publicly displayed and debated. Through a series of elaborate urban displays, such as Henry Dreyfus's Democracity and Norman Bel Geddes's Futurama, the World's Fair played a crucial role in promoting the spatial practices that were subsequently used to reconstruct post-WWII New York City. Not only did the fair provide many New Yorkers with their first exposure to new trends in architecture and urban planning, but it also aggressively promoted those trends through rhetorically powerful exhibits that infused the fair's urban paradigm with a luminous utopian aura. Probing beneath the fair's streamlined façades, however, many cultural representations of the fair have deconstructed the fair's socio-spatial ideology. From science fiction texts such as Eando Binder's "The Rope Trick" and Jack Womack's *Terraplane* to revisionist historical novels such as E. L. Doctorow's *World's Fair* and Miles Beller's *Dream of Venus (Or Living Pictures)*, cultural representations of the fair have frequently explored how the fair promoted cultural xenophobia, corporate ideologies, and a blind faith in techno-rational progress. Analyzing both the fair itself and cultural representations of the fair, this chapter demonstrates the important role that cultural representations of architectural and urban spaces have played both in promoting new spatial practices and in critiquing the ideological significance of those practices. Ultimately, the conflict between the fair and its critics represents, in nascent form, the cultural antagonisms that later emerged between urban planners and the cultural avant-garde in post-WWII New York.

Exploring how similar conflicts replayed themselves a generation later, chapter 2 describes how post-WWII New York writers critically analyzed the social and spatial restructuring of their city. While many New Yorkers eagerly embraced post-WWII American urbanism's turn toward the functionalist geometry of International Style Modernist architecture and urban planning, the post-WWII New York avant-garde strongly opposed these spatial practices on both aesthetic and political grounds. Taking corporate architecture as both a symbolic expression and a material inscription of corporate ideologies, writers such as Allen Ginsberg and George Oppen used negative, ambiguous, and fragmented representations of skyscrapers to deconstruct the skyscraper's—and hence corporate America's—traditional function as the socio-spatial center of American cities. In particular, they critically analyzed how International Style corporate architecture functioned both as a symbolic mirror and an ideological mask by simultaneously revealing and concealing the cultural logic of post-WWII corporate capitalism. As a symbolic expression of corporate culture, International Style Modernism's homogeneous, geometrical spatial aesthetic materially inscribed the "organization man" ideology of post-WWII corporate America onto New York City's architectural and urban spaces. As an ideological mask, however, International Style Modernism's shiny, homogeneous surfaces concealed the more troubling exclusionary and anti-urban logic of post-WWII corporate capitalism. Like the World Fair's streamlined urban utopias, International Style Modernist corporate architecture concealed the contradictory and violent dimensions of the capitalist political economy.

Focusing on how many post-WWII New York writers developed interart aesthetic practices modeled after non-literary cultural forms such as jazz and the visual arts, chapters 3 and 4 analyze how several Beat Generation, Black Arts, and New York School writers used interart aesthetic practices specifically to discuss urban issues. Exploring how jazz influenced post-WWII New York literature, chapter 3 describes how both Beat and Black Arts writers used jazz to represent, analyze, and imagine alternatives to the city's post-WWII restructuring. Either they represented jazz as a counter-hegemonic force that "shivered," "infiltrate[d]," and "attack[ed]" the city, or they described marginal jazz spaces that existed outside—at "*a lower level and a more rapid tempo*" than or "drift[ing] above"—the city's dominant socio-spatial logic (Ginsberg 131; Kaufman, "Battle Report," 110; Ellison 9; Neal 145). In particular, Beat writers turned to the ecstatic, fragmented, and polymorphic "liquid geometry" of bebop jazz to critique the rational, rectilinear "pure geometry" of International Style Modernist architecture and its material inscription of corporate ideologies onto urban space (Hull 87; Corbusier 22). Black Arts writers, however, turned toward the more politicized and Afro-centric styles of hard bop and avant-garde jazz musicians—such as John Coltrane, Charles Mingus, Sun Ra, and Pharoah Sanders—to develop a more politicized critique of urban racial and economic segregation.

Turning from jazz to the visual arts, chapter 4 analyzes how New York School poets experimented with new aesthetic practices that connected their interdisciplinary interest in the visual arts with their critical exploration of the socio-political significance of architectural and urban spaces. While many previous analyses of the New York School have interpreted these poets as either passively translating visual aesthetics practices into textual forms or mechanically imitating the complex rhythms of urban life, I argue that the New York poets' multi-faceted, interdisciplinary aesthetic experiments explore a wide range of "ar(t)chitextural" interrelationships between visual, spatial, and textual practices. Focusing specifically on the work of Barbara Guest and Frank O'Hara, I argue not only that these two writers repeatedly oscillate between exploring visual and spatial themes, but also that it is precisely the interrelationship between their visual and spatial interests—more than either interest in and of itself—that distinguishes many of their successful works. Nevertheless, even though Guest and O'Hara both share a common interest in the interrelationship between visual and spatial forms, they explore this interrelationship in different ways with Guest focusing more exclusively on the visual aesthetics of modernist art while O'Hara explores a broader range of interrelationships between visual and spatial practices.

The larger trajectory of *Deconstructing Post-WWII New York City* oscillates between two seemingly opposed, but intricately interconnected, dimensions of post-WWII New York literature. On the one hand, it continually historicizes post-WWII New York literature within its urban material context. It explores how writers and other artists collectively developed a kind of critical urban discourse about their city's complex socio-spatial topography. On the other hand, it also emphasizes the crucial role that the aesthetic imagination played in the formation, articulation, and evolution of this critical urban discourse. For many writers and artists, post-WWII New York City was not simply a milieu to write about or even a socio-political text to analyze and deconstruct. It also functioned as a kind of aesthetic muse that provided a socio-spatial analogue for the kind of artistic practices that they wanted to create. Consequently, many members of the post-WWII New York avant-garde experimented with new aesthetic strategies that emulated the complexity, heterogeneity, spontaneity, and uncertainty that they found in particular urban spaces. But they were constantly vigilant about how the post-WWII restructuring of their city threatened to destroy both these urban spaces and the kind of urban aesthetic imagination that these spaces helped inspire. Because of this, their work frequently explores various interrelationships between urban and aesthetic themes both by turning to various kinds of urban spaces as models for creating new urban aesthetic practices and by using those aesthetic practices to critically analyze and politically contest the city's socio-spatial restructuring. Bringing together these two material and aesthetic dimensions of post-WWII New York literature, *Deconstructing Post-WWII New York City* demonstrates how the interart aesthetic experiments of the post-WWII New York avant-garde also raise significant social, economic, and political questions about the ideological significance of urban spaces.

Chapter One

Constructing the Post-WWII Megalopolitan Subject

The Socio-Spatial Ideology of the 1939–40 New York World's Fair

The American religion paraded its eschatological predictions and deep utopian faith most memorably and definitively at the 1939 New York World's Fair. The fair was a credo in stucco and steel. . . . As such that World's Fair is important to any credible effort at deciphering modern America. . . . It is essential that we understand Democracity if we are to understand the fair. . . . Democracity's utopian World of Tomorrow amounts, in essence, to the modern suburbs.
—David Gelernter, from *1939: The Lost World of the Fair*

EVEN BEFORE THE START OF WWII, THE SPATIAL PRACTICES THAT WOULD LATER dominate postwar American urbanism were synthesized into a new urban ideology that was "first directly experienced by a broad American audience at the New York World's Fair of 1939–40" (Stern et al., *New York 1960*, 47). Built on land reclaimed from the Corona dump, a 1216–acre urban wasteland described by F. Scott Fitzgerald's *The Great Gatsby* as "a valley of ashes—a fantastic farm where ashes grow like wheat into ridges and hills and grotesque gardens"—the construction of the fairgrounds itself was the "largest single reclamation project ever undertaken in the Eastern United States" (Fitzgerald 27; *Official Guide Book,* 27). Epitomizing late-1930s America's fascination with clean, practical, techno-rational designs, the fair celebrated "designers," "architects," and "engineers" as the "true poets of the twentieth century" (*Official Guide Book,* 29). Its numerous exhibits displayed everything from refrigerators and washing machines to soda shops and industrial production methods redesigned according to futuristic variations on the machine-age aesthetics of late-1930s American modernism. For example, the Transportation Zone displayed sleek Bauhaus-inspired locomotives, streamlined tear-shaped automobiles, and Raymond Loewy's Rocketport, a futuristic simulation of rocket travel. While the Rocketport admitted that rocket flight was "at present impossible," it maintained that the only obstacle preventing it was "almost wholly limited to invention of a proper fuel" (Gerald Wendt, quoted in Gelernter 155). Similarly, Borden Milk's Dairy World of Tomorrow featured a Rotolactor machine that streamlined the milking of cows. Not only did the Rotolactor "electrically" milk five cows at once, but it gently bopped them with an "automatic rear-end bopper" after they were finished (Gelernter 107). The Borden exhibit also sold Mel-o-rols, "highly engineered ice cream cones, flat on the bottom, designed to accept a horizontal cylinder of vanilla, chocolate or strawberry ice cream on top" (Gelernter 107). In this futuristic dream world, the fair projected the techno-rational ideologies and streamlined machine-age aesthetics of late-1930s America onto a "world of tomorrow" that had few limits.

The techno-rational restructuring of urban space played a particularly significant role in the fair's vision of the future. From one end of the fair to the other, fairgoers encountered constant reminders that the fair's "world of tomorrow" was a world of brave new utopian cities. Inside the Theme Center's Perisphere, the fair's geographical and symbolic center, Henry Dreyfus's Democracity synthesized "all of the fair's themes" into a colossal model of a "perfectly integrated, futuristic metropolis," an 11,000 square-mile city of 1.5 million people in the year 2039 (*Official Guide Book,* 44). Utopian urban designs also played a prominent role in Norman Bel Geddes's Futurama, a $6.5 million, 35,738 square-foot diorama of what America might look like in 1960. Simulating how "wondrous changes and improvements . . . in our national highways" might transform the topography of 1960s America, this vast series of dioramas culminated with a spectacular vision of the "many wonders" that could be achieved by "modern and efficient city planning," including "abundant sunshine, fresh air, fine green parkways, recreational and civic centers," and "breath-taking architecture" (General Motors Corporation 5, 17–19). In addition to these two "utopian extravaganzas," which were "fairgoers' first and second favorites," various kinds of urban and suburban spaces were displayed in smaller venues such as Walter Dorwin Teague's City of Light, Willard Van Dyke and Ralph Steiner's documentary *The City,* and the Town of Tomorrow (Gelernter 26). Noting how these urban displays pervaded the fair, Janet Abu-Lughod has argued that it is "amazing to recognize how central 'the city' was to the 1939 vision of tomorrow," while Leonard Wallock has claimed that the fair was "not finally about the land of tomorrow, neither was it about the world at large. Rather, 'the fair was the city's perfected dream of itself'" (Abu-Lughod 186; Wallock 20). Taken collectively, the fair's various architectural and urban displays synthesized a wide range of European and American spatial practices into a more or less coherent urban paradigm that marked "a pivotal moment in the course of world architecture" by articulating "remarkably cohesive messages concerning the American reaction to European Modernism, the triumph of corporation-based industrialism, and the suburbanization of the landscape on a vast scale" (Stern et al., *New York 1930*, 727, 729). In short, the fair was one of the conceptual crucibles in which the socio-spatial ideology of post-WWII American urbanism was forged.

As one of the first significant forums in which this urban ideology was publicly displayed and debated, the fair's urban dioramas provide a necessary frame of reference for understanding the historical evolution of post-WWII American urban history. Tracing a direct genealogical descent from the fair's urban dioramas to the post-WWII restructuring of American cities, David Gelernter not only argues that understanding the fair is "important to any credible effort at deciphering modern America," but he claims more specifically that we must "understand Democracity if we are to understand the fair" because post-WWII American urbanism largely "realized the heart" of Democracity's "utopian World of Tomorrow [which] amounts, in essence, to the modern suburbs" (53, 67, 71). As the initial drafts of what would eventually evolve into the dominant paradigm of post-WWII American urbanism, Democracity, the Futurama, and the fair's other urban displays not only embodied the socio-spatial logic of post-WWII New York City in embryonic form, but they also provoked similar kinds of cultural and political opposition. With the notable exception of David Gelernter's nostalgia-driven historical romance, *1939: The Lost World of the Fair* (1995), cultural representations of the 1939–40 New York World's Fair almost invariably criticize it in ways that bear strong family resemblances to the New York avant-garde's critique of the neo-Corbusian restructuring of post-WWII New York City. Probing beneath the fair's clean, shiny, streamlined surfaces, many cultural representations of the fair expose various cultural and political contradictions in the fair's socio-spatial ideology. They document how the fair's techno-rational designs promoted an illusion of democracy that excluded both ethnic minorities and the economically disenfranchised. They demonstrate how its streamlined, machine-age aesthetics functioned as an ideological mask for the economic and political interests of corporate capitalism. They also turn to the fair's own complex, marginal spaces—such as Salvidor Dalí's Dream of Venus exhibit or the Amusement Area—as models for developing alternative counter-hegemonic spatial, political, and urban agendas.

Examining the fair through a literary perspective, this chapter analyzes how the fair's urban ideology has been represented by cultural texts such as Eando Binder's science-fiction short story, "The Rope Trick" (1939); E. L. Doctorow's semi-autobiographical novel, *World's Fair* (1985); Jack Womack's science-fiction thriller, *Terraplane: A Futuristic Novel of New York, 1939* (1988); David Gelernter's historical romance, *1939: The Lost World of the Fair* (1995); Miles Beller's postmodern historiographic metafiction, *Dream of Venus (Or Living Pictures): A Novel of the 1939 New York World's Fair* (2000); and Matt Groening's satirical comic and television sit-com, *Futurama* (1998—). By representing, analyzing, and imagining alternatives to the fair's urban ideology, these cultural representations of the fair function as a kind of critical urban discourse that not only excavates the archaeological pre-history of post-WWII American urbanism, but also critically deconstructs its dominant socio-spatial ideology. The conflicts that develop between these cultural representations of the fair and the fair itself reflect an incipient late-1930s form of the cultural tensions that subsequently emerged in post-WWII New York City between the city's architects and urban planners and its cultural avant-garde.

Through its numerous, elaborate urban displays, the fair exposed fairgoers to many trends in architecture and urban planning that would subsequently play a dominant role in the post-WWII restructuring of American cities. It also attempted to endow this new urban ideology with a brilliant utopian aura. Fascinated with New York City's newly emerging role as an international capital, Walter Dorwin Teague's City of Light recreated "24 hours in the life of New York portrayed in [a] thrilling 12–minute drama" that allowed fairgoers to watch as "trains speed in subways, elevators rise and descend in skyscrapers, [and] motor traffic flows across suspension bridges" (*Official Guide Book,* 179–80). In addition to encapsulating the city's dynamic rhythms in a miniature form, Teague's City of Light also asserted New York City's importance as a global city. As one advertisement for the exhibit explained, New York City itself was an expression of the future because "no other city ha[d] advanced nearly so far along the road that leads to the world of tomorrow" (*Official Guide Book,* 180). Convinced both that New York City would play a prominent role in defining the world civilization of the future and that the fair would help design the new urban practices that would make this new world civilization possible, the fair's designers envisioned the fair as a place where New York architects and urban planners could "as members of a great metropolis . . . think for the world at large" and "lay the foundation for a pattern of life which would have an enormous impact in times to come" (Lewis Mumford, quoted in Cusker 4). Thus the fair's designers endowed the fair's urban ideology, the ideology that would dominate the spatial restructuring of post-WWII New York City, with a bold utopian significance.

In addition to exalting New York City as a paradigmatic city of the future, the fair also developed bold, futuristic, techno-rational urban utopias that would eventually serve as models for restructuring post-WWII New York City itself. For example, Henry Dreyfus's Democracity synthesized many of the architectural and urban practices displayed at the fair into a new urban design that used a sprawling radial pattern of multi-laned highways to connect a dense urban Centerton with seventy suburban Pleasantvilles and light-industrial Millvilles (Stern et al., *New York 1930*, 752). This new urban design fused the streamlined, machine-age aesthetics of 1930s American modernism with the rectilinear "pure geometry" of avant-garde European architecture, and it also combined Le Corbusier's auto-centric radiant city and Wright's decentralized Broadacre City into a single composite urban form. In addition to synthesizing various trends in architecture and urban planning, Democracity asserted the utopian signifi-cance of its techno-rational urban design through an elaborate rhetorical display. Not only was Democracity centrally located inside the Perisphere, but visitors entered it by ascending the world's longest escalator up to two circular galleries, which rotated in opposite directions around the Perisphere, while the popular radio newscaster, H. V. Kaltenborn, praised "the good life of this well-planned city" (quoted in White 25). After grant-ing fairgoers a brief two-minute glimpse of this utopian city as it passed from dawn to dusk, Democracity's utopian vision was further reinforced by a multi-media extravaganza: the lights were dimmed, and the Perisphere's "celestial concave" was lit up with "myriad stars" while a "symphonic poem, a chorus of a thousand voices reache[d] out of the heavens" and a vision of the "interdependent society of today" was projected overhead:

> at ten equi-distant points in the purple dome loom marching men—farmers, stamped by their garb; mechanics with their tools of trade. As the marchers approach they are seen to represent the various groups in modern society—all the elements that must work together to make possible the better life which would flourish in such a city as lies below. The symphony rises to diapasonal volume, the figures assume mammoth size, and suddenly a blaze of polaroid light climaxes the show. Seldom, if ever, has such an entrancing vista been created by man. (*Official Guide Book*, 45)

Repeated 120 times each day, some 8,000 visitors witnessed this spectacle every hour.

The quasi-religious fervor of Dreyfus's spectacular presentation tech-niques, however, suggests that Democracity performed more significant and more interesting kinds of cultural work than simply presenting new trends in architecture and urban planning. It did "further the public's per-ception of a megalopolitan rather than a metropolitan future" by encapsu-lating "several of the fair's central themes: the viability of creating social order and stability through careful urban planning; a predilection for Streamline architecture and design; and the recognition of the imminent hegemony of the automobile" (Stern et al., *New York 1930*, 752). But the multi-media sound and light show used to present this megalopolitan par-adigm was more propagandistic than techno-rational. As J. P. Tellotte explains, Dreyfus's "five-and-a-half-minute program" was constructed like a "miniature science fiction narrative:" it "implied that such a world 'is possible today,'" yet there was also a fantastic, Hollywood-esque "'dreamy' or 'wishful' aura in those claims, a great distance between those claims and reality" (173). But why did Democracity need a science-fiction melodrama that included "mammoth" marching figures, "blaze[s] of polaroid light," and a "chorus of a thousand voices" rising to "diapasonal volume" to sell its urban vision if that vision was so rational and practical? Democracity may have helped develop and display a new urban design, but its extravagant rhetoric also had an ideological function of helping condition the American public to accept that new urban ideology. Like many of the fair's urban displays, it went well beyond simply designing the cities of the future: it also attempted to construct the new urban subjects who would inhabit those cities. It provided many fairgoers with their first lesson in post-WWII American urbanism, a crash course on the neo-Corbusian radiant skyscraper cities and Broadacre-esque garden suburbs of the future.

Norman Bel Geddes's Futurama also used extravagant, hard-sell marketing techniques to promote its vast "animated panorama of towns and cities, rivers and lakes, country and farm areas, industrial plants in operation, country clubs, forests, valleys and snow-capped mountains" as they were envisioned to be in the 1960s (*Official Guide Book*, 208). Much like the Disney theme-park rides that it later inspired, the Futurama transported fairgoers in "magic" moving chairs equipped with an audio recording that described their journey through "the largest and most realistic scale model ever constructed" (*Official Guide Book*, 208). Riding past this miniaturized world in their "magic" chairs, fairgoers experienced "the sensation of traveling hundreds of miles and viewing scenes from a low-flying airplane" as it flew through time into a futuristic 1960s America where "every type of terrain in America" was integrated within a transcontinental "motor system . . . laid down over the entire country—across mountains, over rivers and lakes, through cities and past towns—never deviating from a direct course" (*Official Guide Book*, 208; Geddes 5). While fairgoers' responses to this vast fantasy world were not entirely involuntary—as evidenced by contemporary commentators, such as David Haskell and E. B. White, who openly criticized both the fair's exhibits and the techniques used to present them—the Futurama aggressively attempted to interpolate fairgoers into its urban ideology. Not only were visitors shuttled through the exhibit as passive spectators in their "magic" chairs, but the chairs themselves were equipped with individual speakers that explained the significance of each image they passed. Even if fairgoers were not completely powerless to resist these ideological instructions, the Futurama's massive scale and elaborate designs, its totalizing perspective of looking down on a miniaturized world, and the tens of thousands of mysteriously enchanted moving cars speeding throughout the exhibit as if it were alive, all enhanced the exhibit's rhetorical power. As General Motors' famous photograph of fairgoers looking down at the Futurama from their "magic" chairs suggests, the display techniques used to present the Futurama were as significant as the urban design that it displayed because those techniques powerfully influenced how fairgoers received and interpolated themselves into the urban ideology being presented to them. They were an integral part of both the exhibit's immense popularity and its broader ideological function, which the architectural critic David Haskell compared to a "vast carburetor, sucking in the crowd by fascination into its feeding tubes, carrying the people throughout the prescribed route, and finally whirling them out, at the very center of the display, so they might drift out in free dispersion" (quoted in Meikle 200). And to top it all, the Futurama literally interpolated its visitors into its urban ideology at the end of the ride. After viewing the Futurama's final intersection, passengers were presented with a button boldly proclaiming, "I Have Seen the Future," and then—as if in fulfillment of the button's prophesy—they were deposited onto the Intersection of Tomorrow, a life-size replica of the last intersection they had just seen at the end of the ride. Thus, the ride not only displayed a futuristic urban model and helped condition visitors to accept that model, but it also allowed them to personally experience its brave new cities firsthand and twenty years ahead of schedule.

Given how much money, work, and attention for detail were lavished on this exhibit, it is not surprising that commentators have repeatedly described it as "easily the smash hit of the Fair" and "the fair's greatest hit" ("Life Goes to the Futurama" 79; Meikle 188). On this point, contemporary literary representations of the fair concur: David Gelernter's *1939: The Lost World of the Fair* describes the Futurama as "the fair's most popular exhibit by far" (25), while E. L. Doctorow's *World's Fair* proclaims it "everyone's first stop," the "most popular in the whole Fair," and the "most fantastic sight I had ever seen, an entire city of the future, with skyscrapers and fourteen-lane highways, real little cars moving on them at different speeds, the center lanes for the higher speeds, the lanes on the edge for the lower" (251–2). In fact, the Futurama was so popular that its designer, Norman Bel Geddes, declared it the biggest tourist attraction of all time:

> Five million people saw the Futurama of the General Motors Highways and Horizons Exhibit at the New York World's Fair during the summer of 1939. In long queues that often stretched more than a mile, from 5,000 to 15,000 men, women and children at a time, stood, all day long every day, under the hot sun and in the rain, waiting more than an hour for their turn to get a sixteen-minute glimpse at the motorways of the world of tomorrow. There have been hit shows and sporting events in the past which had waiting lines for a few days, but never before had

> there been a line as long as this, renewing itself continuously, month after month,
> as there was every day at the Fair. (Geddes 3)

But why did the longest line in world history before 1939 form at this particular spot? What was so enticing about the Futurama and its futuristic
vision of techno-rational cities and highways that it not only attracted a
record-setting crowd in its own day but still continues to dominate contemporary discussion of the fair's historical and cultural significance? Why
has such intense interest been focused on what was essentially a highly
commercialized, hopelessly idealized, and aggressively pedantic representation of the spatial practices of post-WWII American urbanism: rationally
organized techno-fetishist skyscraper cities, radically homogeneous sprawling suburbs, and the streamlined mega-highways that connect them into
vast megalopolitan systems? Moreover, when the Futurama and the fair's
other utopic urban dioramas are placed within a broader historical context,
what do they teach us about how the socio-spatial organization of post-
WWII American cities has so powerfully captured the collective imagination of multiple generations: the postwar generation that produced and
consumed it, the preceding generation that dreamed it into existence and
waited in "long queues that often stretched more than a mile" just to catch
a glimpse of it, and the subsequent generation that now lives in its wake
(Geddes 3)? The remainder of this chapter explores how several cultural
representations of the fair—both from its day and from our own—represent the fair in order to explain, analyze, and critique the socio-spatial ideology of post-WWII American urbanism.

The Futurama's "Vaguely Miesian" Dream Cities: The Urban Ideology of David Gelernter's 1939, The Lost World of the Fair

> Geddes's Futurama took you on an imaginary flight across America from coast to
> coast. . . . You encountered cities of the future along the way: Their skyscrapers
> were thrusting tall boxes with rounded edges and wraparound glass walls, vague-
> ly Miesian. . . . From 1939, 1960 seemed like a brilliant, glittering dream. And
> looking back, 1960 was a brilliant glittering dream. The fair kept its promises. So
> many of its predictions came true.
> —David Gelernter, from *1939: The Lost World of the Fair*

As the contemporary novel that most enthusiastically espouses the fair's
own ideology, David Gelernter's historical romance, *1939: The Lost World
of the Fair*, represents the hermeneutic horizon of the late-1930s architects
and industrial designers who designed the fair. Like Howard Roark in Ayn
Rand's *The Fountainhead*, Gelernter's protagonist, Mark Handler, is an
"idealistic" engineer-architect who is "passionate about architecture and
believe[s] it to be—how would he have put it?—the defining artistic medi-

um of modern times" (42, 140). He endlessly discusses the dominant intellectual trends of his day, and he has a particular passion for the architectural theories of "Corbusier, Wright, who was just coming back into fashion—Mark had always admired him; Raymond Hood, Eric Mendelsohn,
Ely Jacques Kahn" (142). In addition to situating the fair within this intellectual milieu, Gelernter's novel also describes how the fair's urban ideology reflected a general interest in redesigning urban spaces. In particular, it
emphasizes how appealing the fair must have been to a generation that was
just emerging from the Depression and attempting to build a hopeful
"world of tomorrow" on a scale comparable to the WPA's New Deal development projects. Gelernter repeatedly reminds his contemporary readers
how we now have the luxury to "take the 'marriage of town and country'
for granted, and when 1939 gets excited about it, we shrug our shoulders.
It's not utopia, we point out, it's just suburbia" (71). To this casual dis-
missal of suburbia, Gelernter replies with the voice of post-Depression
America: "It looks a lot like utopia to us, says 1939. Utopia is a place
where, for vast numbers of people, life all in all is pretty good" (71).
Gelernter explicitly identifies the "fundamental divide between our world
view and the high thirties'" by "our respective canonical views of Robert
Moses" and his Haussmann-esque approach to urban redevelopment:
while our generation of post-Jane Jacobs, post-Robert Caro critics gives a
critical "thumbs-down on Moses," previous generations lauded him as a
"master builder" (78). Consequently, contemporary America now feels
"little sense of control over the landscape" and the "act of building comes
hard to us," while late-1930s America "had a deep sense of control over
the American landscape . . . derived at least in part from throwing dams
and bridges across rivers, digging tunnels and raising tall buildings"
(273–4). Situating the fair within these intellectual and historical contexts,
Gelernter argues that the fair's urban ideology represented a populist "*cri
de coeur*" that "had a certain urgent importance" in its day (47). From the
perspective of late-1930s America, the Futurama's "vaguely Miesian" techno-fetishist architecture and auto-centric "cities of the future" seemed like
a "brilliant glittering dream" (23–4). Similarly, Van Dyke and Steiner's doc-
umentary, *The City*, might have "hated" cities and viewed them as little
more than "noise and fumes and shouts and shrillness and ambulances,
drunks, fire trucks, stuck in traffic, angry cops," but this anti-urban bias
makes more sense in its historical context (Gelernter 68). After viewing Van
Dyke and Steiner's gritty depictions of the polluted and impoverished
streets of Depression-era Pittsburgh, their idealization of suburban life
seems more understandable.

By emphasizing how the fair's urban utopias expressed a "deep strain
of optimism among fairgoers themselves," Gelernter's novel also attempts
to legitimize the post-WWII restructuring of American cities (27).

According to Gelernter, 1960 not only "seemed like a brilliant, glittering dream" from the perspective of 1939, but "looking back, 1960 *was* a brilliant glittering dream. The fair kept its promises. So many of its predictions came true" (27). After the end of WWII, both the corporations that paid millions of dollars to build the fair's urban dioramas and the public that waited in mile-long lines to see them were more than willing to reconstruct New York City in the fair's image of brave new utopian cities. Corporations touted "anonymously detailed, blandly profiled, bulky" International Style glass-and-steel boxes as "proud corporate symbols," while post-WWII New Yorkers were "launched into ecstatic transports" by Levittown with more than a million of them fleeing to the suburbs by the end of the 1950s (Stern et al., *New York 1960*, 53; Gelernter 67). Moving seamlessly between praising Geddes's Futurama as a "brilliant, glittering dream" that "far transcended the profit interests of GM" and valorizing post-WWII American urbanism as the fair's "utopian promises [come] true," Gelernter argues that the fair's urban ideology not only "had a certain urgent importance" but it "*still* does" (24–5, 47, 49). Thus, Gelernter's historical fiction simultaneously idealizes the fair's urban ideology and legitimizes post-WWII American urbanism for realizing the "heart" of that utopian ideology (71). The novel's larger rhetorical purpose, therefore, lies not simply in how it recreates the historical context of the 1939–40 New York World's Fair, but rather in how it uses the hermeneutic horizon of the fair's designers to justify post-WWII American urbanism. It turns back to the fair both to excavate the historical origins of post-WWII American urbanism and to create a narrative perspective that, like the fair itself, largely masks the cultural and political contradictions of the urban ideology that it advocates. Like Democracity and the Futurama, Gelernter's novel simultaneously describes a particular urban ideology and attempts to interpolate its readers into that ideology: it tries to reconstruct contemporary urban subjects who will conform to the socio-spatial ideology that the fair shares with post-WWII American urbanism.

The immense popularity of the fair's urban displays alone, however, is not sufficient to establish either Gelernter's claim that the "fair was no mere anthology of corporate America" or his contention that post-WWII American urbanism largely fulfilled the fair's "utopian promises" (25, 49). While it is indisputable that both the fair's urban dioramas and post-WWII American urbanism have been extremely popular, at least among certain segments of the population, they have also been critically analyzed and politically opposed by others. Like the fair's dream cities, post-WWII American urbanism did extend the benefits of technological progress and economic prosperity to a wider audience, but it did so in ways that were both racially and economically discriminatory. It extended the American dream to more people through federal housing and highway subsidies, but virtually all of its new urban and suburban spaces, from Levvittown to Stuyvesant Town, were racially segregated. The Futurama and Democracity neither acknowledged nor attempted to redress these kinds of racial issues. Just as the fair presented a brave new vision of the "world of tomorrow," but only to those who could afford its steep admission fees and concession charges, post-WWII American urbanism also enabled the predominantly white middle-class to "escape" a little farther from the city while "trapping" other lower-class and racial minorities within embattled inner-city ghettos. By not seriously addressing the racial and economic contradictions of either the fair or post-WWII American urbanism, Gelernter's historical fiction obscures how the fair's utopian promises were both selectively made and selectively fulfilled.

Moreover, Gelernter's repeated claim that the fair represented more than "blatant consumerism," "profit interests," or an "anthology of corporate America" seems to protest too much (46, 25). Gelernter has a point, but by asserting that point too strongly he obscures the equally significant corporate dimensions of both the fair and post-WWII American urbanism. Instead of exploring how the fair's complex, heterogeneous topography oscillated between visionary utopianism and corporate propaganda, Gelernter paints a one-dimensional picture of the fair. By minimizing the fair's corporate dimension, he also redirects attention away from how the fair displayed its new urban ideology and attempted to interpolate urban subjects into that ideology. Consequently, Gelernter repeatedly represents the fair's urban dioramas as simply expressing an already existent, widespread, popular desire for their utopian urbanism without adequately considering how the fair's spectacular urban simulacra also helped construct and produce that desire. When Gelernter's character, Hattie Glassman, recollects her own experience of the Futurama, however, what she remembers is the exhibit's elaborate rhetorical construction: how you "filed in through a tall, narrow slit;" how the "letters *GM* flank[ed] the cleft and the ramps enter[ed] between them;" how the "brilliant color, and motion" of its "snaked ramps" contrasted against its "blank cliff-like wall;" how you were "plopped down in a tall, cushioned seat, very comfortable;" how each chair "had its own piped-in sound track with music and narration;" how these chairs "travel[ed] smoothly and ke[pt] level over the twisting and turning, rising, falling track;" how you "got the lovely feeling of eavesdropping from your box seat as you winged it over the futuristic landscape;" and how the "end was enormously clever" (19–22). For Hettie, the Futurama itself—even more than the urban ideology it displayed—was "one virtuoso piece of thirties engineering" (21). It is left almost entirely to Gelernter's narrator to describe, explain, and justify the Futurama's utopian urban ideology. By splitting the narrative between Hettie's emotional reaction to the exhibit's intricate rhetorical construction and the narrator's political interest in the exhibit's utopian ideology, Gelernter inadvertently demonstrates the opposite of what he claims: the Futurama's spectacular display techniques influenced fairgoers like Hettie more dramatically than its architectural and urban ideology did. What "sold" the fair's urban ideology was not only its techno-rational engineering but also the extravagant imagine-ering that designed the display techniques used to interpolate fairgoers into the exhibit's ideology. While Gelernter repeatedly disavows these exclusionary and ideological dimensions of the fair, they were readily apparent to many of the fair's contemporary critics, ranging from E. B. White and Albert Einstein to science-fiction writers such as Eando Binder. Gelernter's historical romance might faithfully recreate the hermeneutic horizon of the fair's designers, but it does not adequately probe how that hermeneutic horizon masked deep-rooted political and cultural conflicts in late-1930s American culture—conflicts that were not only recognized by many of the fair's contemporary critics but also plainly manifested and widely discussed when the fair's urban ideology was later used to reconstruct post-WWII American cities.

"[W]E MUST BUILD THEM THE HIGHWAYS SO THEY CAN SELL US THE CARS": DECONSTRUCTING THE FAIR'S CORPORATE IDEOLOGY

> I liked 1960 in purple light, going a hundred miles an hour around impossible turns ever onward toward the certified cities of the flawless future. It wasn't till I passed an apple orchard and saw the trees, each blooming under its own canopy of glass, that I perceived that even the General Motors dream, as dreams so often do, left some questions unanswered about the future. The apple tree of tomorrow, abloom under its inviolate hood, makes you stop and wonder. How will the little boy climb it? Where will the little bird build its nest?
> —E. B. White, from "They Come with Joyous Song"

In his dedication of the Palestine Pavilion at the 1939–40 New York World's Fair, Albert Einstein criticized how the fair "project[ed] the world of men like a wishful dream" by exhibiting modern civilization's "creative forces" while hiding its "sinister and destructive ones which today more than ever jeopardize the happiness, the very existence of civilized humanity." Einstein's criticism seems much more cognizant of the fair's complex position within a twentieth-century world where techno-rational ideologies were already breaking down into fascism, genocide, world war, and nuclear destruction. Like Einstein, E. B. White's review of the fair for *The New Yorker* also explored the ideological contradictions and complexities that the fair attempted to cover over with its futuristic facades. Criticizing the Futurama's vision of "1960 in purple light, going a hundred miles an hour around impossible turns ever onward toward the certified cities of the flawless future," White described the Futurama as a dream world that "as dreams often do, left some questions unanswered about the future" (26). He questioned whether there would be room for nature, pleasure, culture, and human emotions in the fair's brave new utopian cities. He also described the fair's "road to tomorrow" as a "long familiar journey" through corporate America's "Mulsified Shampoo and Mobilgas, through Bliss Street, Kix, Astring-O-Sol, and the Majestic Auto Seat Cover" (25). For White, the fair seemed to be "merely Heinz jousting with Beech-Nut— the same old contest on a somewhat larger field, with accommodations for more spectators, and rather better facilities all around" (25). As these descriptions demonstrate, even in its own day many critics complained that the fair attempted to conceal the complexities and contradictions of late 1930s-America's dream-world of technological and economic "progress."

The first literary representation of the World's Fair, Eando Binder's 1939 science-fiction short story, "Rope Trick," presents a similar critique of the fair's one-dimensional utopian ideology. Describing two time-travelers' voyage to the year 2039, it depicts a futuristic New York City that had realized many of the fair's predictions, including massive "two hundred fifty stor[y]" skyscrapers, multi-tiered "elevated traffic spans," and the "superhighways they vaguely planned in 1939" (81, 77). Like Einstein, however, Binder's story critically analyzes the fair by having each character offer conflicting appraisals of its futuristic utopia. While Doc describes 2039 New York City as a "magnificant, glorious, breathtaking . . . won-der-city of the future" where "[a]ll the things we dreamed of in 1939 have come true," Breckenridge sees it as the "[s]ame old world . . . in more ways than one" (81, 83, 86). In particular, Breckenridge argues that the future "ain't so hot" because these "times may have a few things over our times, but they ain't no justice" (83). He recognizes how the techno-rational achievements of 2039 New York City are overshadowed by what Einstein described as the "sinister and destructive" underside of modern civiliza-tion: omnipresent surveillance systems, robot police forces, and the "[s]ame old world" where "they ain't no justice" (86, 83). While "Rope Trick" is the only literary representation of the fair from its own day, H. Bruce Franklin has pointed out that many of the other science-fiction "stories about Earth's future found in the 1939 *Astounding* challenged" the "uncritical enthusiasm for technological progress . . . projected by the large corporations" at the World's Fair (117). They tended to represent the streamlined aesthetics and techno-rational ideologies of late-1930s American modernism not as a historical reality but rather as a "monu-mental display of all the contradictions" of its age (Franklin 117). As these alternative accounts of the fair demonstrate, Gelernter's historical fiction might situate the fair within a historical context, but the context that it locates the fair in, like the fair itself, reflects a reductive, one-dimensional view of late-1930s America.

Jack Womack's *Terraplane: A Futuristic Novel of New York, 1939* also develops an alternative historical description of late-1930s America by sending twenty-first-century African American and Russian time travelers back to New York City in 1939. Representing different racial and political ideologies than those of the fair's designers, these characters frequently point out late-1930s America's racist and exploitative practices, such as its xenophobia, ethnic violence, legalized segregation, and prejudiced legal system. At the same time, however, Womack's dehumanized, violent, futuristic characters—who kill people as if they were just "fixing breakfast"—also critique late-1930s America's techno-rational metanarratives by depicting the kind of streamlined subjects that those narratives might ultimately produce after playing out to their final terminus (216). When one of Womack's characters is confronted about his lack of feelings, he defends himself by claiming that he has "[s]treamlined them away" because "you get along easier without them" (190). By plotting an alternative, dystopic history of twentieth-century America that extends from the racially segregated streets of 1939 New York City to futuristic, dehumanized extensions of twentieth-century America's military-industrial complex, Womack challenges the fair's utopian ideology. Binder's and Womack's science-fiction narratives demonstrate that there are other ways to describe both the historical context and the historical trajectory of late-1930s American modernism. Streamlining may be efficient, but what kind of efficiency does it produce in the end, and at what cost to whom? Techno-rational urban spaces and subjects may eliminate certain kinds of urban blight, but they do so in a selective manner that serves powerful economic, political, and cultural interests.

The difference between Gelernter's utopic interpretation of the fair and Binder's and Womack's dystopic interpretations is further illustrated by comparing the techno-rational, streamlined, utopian time capsule that Westinghouse Corporation buried at the 1939–40 New York World's Fair with Matt Groening's postmodern parody of that time capsule in the first issue of his comic book *Futurama*. Westinghouse's techno-rational time capsule buried a wide range of representative cultural artifacts from 1930s America in a specially designed metal-alloy intended to preserve the capsule for 5,000 years. In addition, Westinghouse Corporation produced some 20,000 multi-lingual Books of Record that contained directions explaining how to locate its time capsule, and these books were distributed to thousands of libraries and cultural institutions throughout the world in hopes that they might help some distant civilization to discover its time capsule. In sharp contrast to this rationally engineered, and heroically optimistic, act of trans-historical communication, Groening's parody depicts Fry, a "cryogenically-frozen 20th-century pizza delivery boy, thawed out in the year 3000," accidentally uncovering a "Partridge Family lunchbox" that contains cultural miscellany from 1970s America: Kool-Aid packets, Viewmaster reels, Play-Doh, comic books, a Beta-version *Valley of the Dolls* video, an eight-track tape of the *Saturday Night Fever* soundtrack, and a copy of the *New York Times* with headlines about Three Mile Island (1, 4). As this selection of artifacts demonstrates, Groening has much less faith in the fruits of twentieth-century America's techno-rational culture than the 1939–40 New York World's Fair did. In his time capsule, technology is represented by nuclear melt down and the "plastic" consumer and cultural products of 1970s America: Kool–Aid and the Bee-Gees. It's not quite the utopia imagined by the fair, or then again maybe it is, but it is certainly interpreted differently by Groening and his Generation X cohorts who now live inside of it.

Groening's parody also illustrates how drastically hermeneutic horizons change in response to new historical contexts. While Fry covets his new-found cultural treasures, which he believes "can give you a lot of insight into what influenced the 20th century," his futuristic companions question why anyone would "want to do *that*," and they dismiss his artifacts as a "bunch of junk" and "archaic crap from the 20th century" (4–5). Not only do the cultural treasures of one historical period prove inconsequential to another—with Groening's parodic time capsule showing about the same disrespect for Westinghouse Corporation's time capsule as Fry's companions show for his Partridge Family lunch box—but the very concept of historicity itself changes dramatically between the two historical periods. While the Westinghouse time capsule envisions history in terms of thousand-year epochs, Groening's represents twenty-five-year old cultural artifacts as hopelessly outdated. Moreover, by extending this acceleration of historical change a thousand years into the future, Groening questions whether cultural artifacts will be capable of meaningfully communicating across such vast temporal distances or whether future civilizations might simply dismiss history altogether as "archaic crap" (4). Fry's Beta video and eight-track tape are already virtually unreadable, even to contemporary readers only a few decades in the future, let alone to Fry's thousand-year distant companions who are more interested in trans-planetary travel, inter-galactic aliens, and robots. Later in the narrative, this incommunicability becomes downright dangerous when Fry procures some sea monkeys from a curio shop peddling twentieth-century Americana, and these sea monkeys mutate into King Kong-sized jumbo shrimp that almost destroy the futuristic city of New New York. This destructive mutation calls into question whether acts of trans-historical communication and exchange will continue to be either viable or beneficial as we speed forward into an accelerating future—a future represented and promoted by Geddes's Futurama, but questioned and critiqued by Groening's *Futurama*. That Fry is ultimately able to stop the mutant sea monkeys by redeeming the money-back guarantee that accompanied their purchase does nothing to shore up Groening's cautionary tale against the ruins of time, since we know that trans-historical communications and exchanges do not come with such guarantees: only ephemeral consumer products do. Moreover, in the same way that Groening's time capsule explicitly parodies the techno-rational ideology of the Westinghouse time capsule, the entire tone and structure of Groening's *Futurama* deconstructs the fair's broader metanarratives about techno-industrial design, corporate capitalism, and utopic urbanism by depicting a dystopic New New York dominated by corporations, such as Planet Express, which produce weapons of intergalactic destruction and mercilessly exploit their workers in a techno-fetishistic, hyper-radiant city even more dehumanized than our own.

While Groening's parody deconstructs the fair from the comfortable distance of the thirtieth century, E. L. Doctorow develops a similar critique of the fair even within its own historical context. Like Groening, Doctorow also critically analyzes the construction of the Westinghouse time capsule in order to critique the fair's ethnocentric contradictions. While even Westinghouse itself appreciated, though not as much as Groening does, the difficulty of communicating across five millennia, it was oblivious to the fact that its time capsule could not even communicate across the racial, cultural, socio-economic, and geopolitical divides of its own historical present. Despite their meticulous efforts to choose representative artifacts from 1930s America, the artifacts that they included in their time capsule were ethnocentrically selective. As one of Doctorow's characters points out, the Westinghouse time capsule contained nothing about the:

> great immigrations that had brought Jewish and Italian and Irish people to America or nothing to represent the point of view of the workingman: "There is no hint from the stuff they included that America has a serious intellectual life, or Indians on reservations or Negroes who suffer from race prejudice. Why is that?" (284)

For Edgar's father, the answer is obvious: the fair's techno-rationalist ideology concealed the fragmented, contradictory, damaged socio-spatial topography of its own day by projecting over-idealized representations of rationally organized, homogeneous social spaces onto the cities of the future. In designing the futuristic techno-rational world of tomorrow, the fair seems to have continued America's past traditions of erasing its native peoples, working classes, and ethnic and racial minorities from the picture.

To rectify this socio-spatial white-washing of history, Doctorow concludes his novel by having its teenage protagonist, Edgar, bury his own, alternative time capsule which included items that he selected:

to represent to the future my life as I had lived it: my Tom Mix Decoder badge with the spinner shaped like a pistol. My hand-written four-page biography of the life of Franklin Delano Roosevelt, for which I had gotten a grade of 100. This had to be rolled like a cigar. My M. Hohner Marine Band harmonica in its original box that was Donald's but which he had given me when he got the larger model. Two Tootsy Toy lead rocket ships, from which all the paint had been worn, to show I had foreseen the future. My little book, *Ventriloquism Self-Taught*, not because I had succeeded but because I had tried. And finally something I was embarrassed to let Arnold see, a torn silk stocking of my mother's, badly run, and which she had thrown away and I had recovered; as an example of the kind of textiles we used—although it was true I had heard that women no longer wore silk stockings in protest against the Japanese, but now wore cotton or that new nylon stuff made of chemicals. (287-8)

Just before Edgar buries his time capsule, however, his friend Arnold adds to it his "old prescription pair of eyeglass" with a "cracked" frame because they might show future generations "something about our technology when they look through the lenses" (288). As this alternative time capsule demonstrates, the actual socio-spatial topography of late-1930s America was more fractured than the fair's ideology admitted. The utopian ideology that the fair projected derived from a "cracked" technological perspective that ignored and suppressed the contradictions of its age: the escalating technologies of war that were rapidly spreading from the Nazis in Europe to their "Japanese" allies in the Pacific and the rapidly expanding capitalist consumer culture that carried traces of the "pistols" that "tamed" America's heterogeneous native peoples and natural resources into a homogeneous nation.

When Doctorow's novel turns to the fair's utopian urban dioramas, it finds similar contradictions lurking beneath their futuristic cities of "modern streamlined curvilinear buildings" and "fourteen-lane highways, [with] real little cars moving on them at different speeds" (252). Stepping back from this "splendid panoply of highways," Edgar's dad comments:

"It is a wonderful vision, all those highways and all those radio-driven cars. Of course, highways are built with public money," he said after a moment. "When the time comes, General Motors isn't going to build the highways, the federal government is. With money from us taxpayers." He smiled. "So General Motors is telling us what they can expect from us: we must build them the highways so they can sell us the cars." (285)

So much for the utopian facade of the fair's brave new, techno-rational—i.e., federally-subsidized, auto-centric, corporate—cities of tomorrow. Like Groening's parodic comic strip, Doctorow's revisionist history also deconstructs the socio-political contradictions and corporate interests that the fair's streamlined metanarrative of techno-rational progress attempted to conceal.

The Future will be "as American as Coca-Cola": The "goddam battle zone" of Miles Beller's *Dream of Venus*

> And when the seat finally clicked back into place, Zeke and the other voyagers were face-to-face with an intersection in Adams City, a major U.S. metropolis of 1960. Though the future belongs to all, Bel Geddes and his crew had little doubt it would be as American as Coca-Cola, Kelvinator, and Buster Brown shoes; from Malibu to Mali a planet cast in Hollywood's image animated by one-line epiphanies minted by Madison Avenue. . . . Futurama was a stage set, an elaborately expensive one, nothing more than an entertainment.
> —Miles Beller, from *Dream of Venus (Or Living Pictures)*

While Binder, Doctorow, Womack, and Groening use irony, parody, dystopian science-fiction, and revisionist historiography to deconstruct the fair, Miles Beller's experimental novel, *Dream of Venus (Or Living Pictures): A Novel of the 1939 New York World's Fair*, develops a no-holds-barred, postmodern, meta-historical critique of the fair's techno-rational ideology. Not hiding behind any subtleties, Beller's novel immediately announces its postmodern intentions even before we are introduced to its protagonist, Zeke Lichtenquist, a proto-Pop Artist named after Roy Lichtenstein and James Rosenquist who works as a caricature artist at the World's Fair and has loose connections to the New York avant-garde. After its obligatory postmodern *caveat lector*—"this book is an invention from its forward to its bibliography"—the novel opens with a series of pseudo-historical references and Borgesian false-citations that describe fictitious details about the fair as if they were historically accurate(ix). At the end of this pseudo-historical textual maze, the novel proper begins, "*STOP THE THIEVING BASTARD!*," and proceeds to describe a thief burglarizing an "apoplectic" fat woman "sprawled across the multicolored pavement of the Court of Peace" (1). Meanwhile, mist from the Fountain of Plenty dissolves a tabloid "photograph of a beaming FDR cuddled by a young woman squeezed into metallic shorts with spiky fabric 'sunrays' and a conical bra, 'posterity' emblazoned on each projectile," while a "sailor in civies" watches passively as he tosses the wrapper from his "powdery stick of Wrigley's Spearmint ('A healthfully delicious treat for young folks and grown-ups alike!')" into a "garbage can by Walter Dorwin Teague that mimicked the profile of a speeding Bauhaus train" (1). By revealing the often unacknowledged "thieving" violence, "fat" consumerism, "powdery" corporate interests, and "metallic" and "conical" sexuality that lurked beneath the fair's streamlined facades, Beller deconstructs the "multicolored" utopian ideology of "Peace," "Plenty," and "speeding Bauhaus train[s]" that the fair projected onto its futuristic "world of tomorrow."

Turning away from the fair's exhibits themselves, Beller's novel critically analyzes how and why those exhibits were displayed to the public. In particular, it criticizes the extravagant display techniques that the Futurama used to interpolate fairgoers into its urban ideology. Chasing the thief into the Futurama's "fabricated future," Zeke is "deposited into the gaping maw of Futurama's conjured World of 1960" (16). Instead of explicating the soicio-spatial logic of the exhibit's utopian urban diorama, however, Beller satirizes its "strong and secure, omnipotent, invincible" rhetorical propaganda (16). He lampoons its pedantic techno-rational description of farmers as "agricultural engineers;" he satirizes its hyper-encyclopedic inclusion of "everything from dog turds to super stadia, from wash drying in the breeze to thunderstorms unleashed on downtown dirigible ports;" and he ridicules its utopian depiction of modern man going "the Almighty one better, delivering Eden through farsighted 'municipal engineering' and snappy product design" (16–17). For Gelernter, the Futurama "spoke with authority" in a "deep, portentous narrator's voice," but stripping the Futurama of its "faux stone floors, chrome-plated walls, and corporate claims of 'educational tools for the young," Beller reinterprets it as a "multi-leveled lie, a conspiracy of design and architecture," a "manufactured tomorrow," and an "expensive spook house, a ghost ride for adults" (Gelernter 11–12; Beller 20–21). Like the rest of the fair, the Futurama is "not prompted by high-blown ideals" but rather by nothing "more than commerce American-style" (8, 173). It is an elaborately constructed display, not of a bold new utopian urban paradigm, but of a crass commercial advertisement for General Motors cars. It makes dramatic utopian promises about "THE DAWN OF A NEW AGE . . . THE PROMISE FULFILLED . . . LIFE IN 1960!," but its "airstream moderne version of Coney Island" simply masks its primary objective of selling cars by "defer[ing] our current emotional needs by 'futurizing' them into products and commodities, packaging them and putting them on the shelf called 'feelings' until another day" (13, 20, 153). It uses hard-sell advertising techniques to cathect fairgoers' emotional energies onto the "futuristic" commodities that it displays: cars, mega-highways, and neo-Corbusian radiant cities. Beneath the Futurama's utopian urbanism lurks not only the corporate interests that produced it both to sell cars and to encourage publicly-funded highway construction (in order to sell more cars), but also the proto-Disney, multimedia marketing extravaganza that was used to promote those corporate interests. The Futurama might have displayed an elaborate model of the "vaguely Miesian" radiant cities of the future, but the larger cultural work that it performed was to interpolate fairgoers into an auto-centric world view that served General Motors' corporate interests.

Thus, Beller's postmodern critique of the fair resembles Jane Jacob's critique of post-WWII American urbanism because both critiques focus specifically on how techno-rational urban ideologies are grounded in what Jacobs describes as the "dishonest mask of pretended order, achieved by ignoring or suppressing the real order that is struggling to exist and to be served" (15). As Zeke explains, some people "willingly surrendered to the fair's soaring architecture," "epic statuary," and "confident murals" as "ironclad guarantees of safe-'n'-easy deliverance from spiritual needs and material wants by that panacea furnished by Science," but Zeke himself rejects the fair's utopian urbanism as a series of "dishonest masks" (Beller 7; Jacobs 15). Beller repeatedly describes the fair as a "carny come-on stuccoed onto pasteboard and chicken-wire," a "parlor prank," the "perpetuation of an illusion," a "multi-leveled lie," and a "manufactured tomorrow" (Beller 7, 20–1). Each of these images emphasizes how the fair's pretended order conceals a more complex understanding of both the fair's socio-spatial ideology and, by extension, post-WWII American urbanism. Removing the fair's deceptive façades, Beller depicts the fair as a "goddam battle zone:" a heterotopic space in which the fair's urban utopias, techno-rational metanarratives, and streamlined machine-age aesthetics co-mingle and compete with numerous baser interests, ranging from the violent lawlessness of "*THEIVING BASTARD[S]*," the profit motives of "clanging moolah," and the "WAR CLOUDS DARKENING EUROPE" to consumer goods, "advertising," "pious platitudes," and the "mindless fun" of "baggy-pants vaudevillians and saggy-tit grinders, hustling for a buck" (1–26). On virtually every page of the novel, the fair's utopian spaces press up against, rub shoulders with, and compete with the un-streamlined and un-streamlinable spaces of late-1930s America: the social spaces that the fair ignores and suppresses. The Lagoon of Nations, which is intended to reflect international harmony, is where Zeke hawks souvenir caricatures in front of a discarded newspaper proclaiming the outbreak of WWII. Walter Dorwin Teague's Bauhaus garbage can provides a receptacle for discarded trash. The Fountain of Plenty, The Court of Peace, and statues of the fair's sacred trinity—Art, Science, and Politics—provide the scene for a crime. By self-consciously juxtaposing these seemingly contradictory spaces, Beller forces the reader to confront how the fair's techno-rational ideology concealed a wide range of social and political contradictions: its progressive engineering masked its regressive politics, its utopian ideologies served corporate interests, and its techno-rational ideologies were promoted by ideological propaganda.

Beller's Zeke also explores how the fair's various marginalized spaces—its peep shows, consumption zones, amusement rides, and entertainment palaces—reveal the "gorgeous lesion[s] on the face of tomorrow" by exposing the fair's non-streamlined hedonist, materialist, and sexual

Dream of Venus. Exhibit at the 1939–40 New York World's Fair designed by Salvador Dalí. Carl Van Vechten. 1939. (Reprinted by permission of the Museum of the City of New York)

dimensions (67). In particular, Beller titles his novel after one of Zeke's favorite sites, Salvador Dalí's Dream of Venus, whose "up-yours" surrealist "writhing architecture" placed semi-naked women dressed in mermaid fishtails in a "lopsided landscape" of "sea spikes and ridges" where they "swayed inside tanks dense with seaweed" and played "badminton with dead blowfish" while accompanied by recorded "hysterics of slaughterhouse steers scream[ing] from speakers shaped like pus watches" (65, 67). In the fair's streamlined world of tomorrow this exhibit presented a labyrinthine spatial enigma that confused most fairgoers and cultural commentators, who often referred to it as "20,000 Legs Under the Sea" when they acknowledged it at all. But what exactly was this surrealistic space doing in the fair's utopian world of tomorrow? What alternative socio-spatial ideology did it express, and how did it display that ideology to fairgoers? What kind of cultural work did it perform and for whom?

Unlike the fair's central exhibits—such as the Futurama, Democracity, City of Light, and the Trylon and Perisphere—Dalí's Dream of Venus attempted to expose and fragment, rather than conceal and consolidate, the complexities and contradictions of both the fair and its late-1930s historical context. By producing such an alternative, contradictory, and fragmented space, it helped de-program fairgoers who were being interpolated into the fair's streamlined socio-spatial ideology. Rejecting the fair's metanarrative of techno-rational progress, Dalí's unstreamlined "industrial population of gashing devices sparking and arching" presented an alternative, postmodern anti-metanarrative "without achievement, without reason, without a future" (72–73). It carried on with a "worthless frenzy" and a "demented hunger, a show of excess that ridiculed the pastorale machine age of GM's Futurama and its Good Housekeeping corporate Eden" (73). One of the post-WWII New York avant-garde's principal cultural achievements was to transform the fragmented textual and spatial practices of European modernism into more radically decentered postmodern aesthetic strategies, and Beller titles his novel after and associates his protagonist with Dalí's surrealist fun house precisely because it provides a spatial model for the kind of deconstructive postmodern narrative that Beller's novel develops. Consequently, Dalí's Dream of Venus provides a prototype for the complex aesthetic strategies that the post-WWII New York avant-garde developed to deconstruct the neo-Corbusian restructuring of post-WWII New York City. The opposition between the fair's techno-rational urban dioramas and Dalí's surrealistic architecture not only illustrates an incipient form of the cultural antagonisms that subsequently emerged in post-WWII New York City, but it also helps demonstrate how the historical evolution of the post-WWII New York avant-garde was intimately connected to an on-going intellectual discussion about the nature of both space in general and urban space in particular.

The 1939 New York World's Fair was a quintessential expression of late-1930s America's techno-rational, streamlined, machine-age culture, and its most comprehensive articulation of that cultural zeitgeist could be found in its utopian urban dioramas such as Futurama and Democracity. At the same time, however, there were significant gaps between the fair's streamlined narrative of late-1930s America and the actual complexity of its historical context—both at home and abroad. As David Nye explains, the fair was:

> not a microcosm of 1930s America, but a corporate vision of what the future could be. Much is missing from the era of the New Deal, and the fair is at best a problematic symbol of American culture in the 1930s. Its themes, architecture, and organization lay entirely in the hands of an economic and cultural elite. (104-5)

The fair itself functioned as kind of narrative: it selected, deleted, arranged, and—to use Hayden White's term—"emplotted" a particular story about late-1930s America. That this narrative was filtered through both the generic conventions of science fiction and fairground spectacle and the political perspective of an "economic and cultural elite" beholden to corporate interests, should give us further cause to analyze how much the fair's streamlined metanarrative revealed, and how much it concealed, the late-1930s America that it purported to represent.

Consequently, the fair needs to be reinterpreted not as the "ecstatic closing vision" of some American Golden Age but rather as a "goddam battle zone" where diverse and conflicting forces competed against each other (Gelernter 53, Beller 22). It did develop the utopian urbanism described by Gelernter, but its "false, perfect World of Tomorrow fixed inside Futurama" at least partially functioned as a "deceptive mask of pretended order" that was "achieved by ignoring or suppressing the real order that [was] struggling to exist" beneath it: a non-streamlined and non-streamlinable world extending beyond the "pure geometry" of the fair's new urban utopias (Beller 23; Jacobs 15). Unlike the Futurama's "false, perfect" world, this real order included the working-class and unemployed Americans who could not afford the fair's middle-class admission prices, let alone General Motors latest streamlined automobiles. It also included a wider range of diverse national, cultural, and racial traditions, including Jewish people who were being marginalized at home and destroyed abroad, African Americans who would be asked to fight abroad but stay in their place at home, and Native Americans whose displacement onto reservations provided a tragic prototype for the gentrification, ghettoization, and suburbanization that would restructure post-WWII American cities. None of these groups, however, were accounted for in the fair's streamlined metanarratives. They were not represented in its Futuramas, Homes of Tomorrow, and time capsules. They were given few opportunities for employment at the fair, and even those opportunities were mostly menial jobs. As Oliver P. Rivert, an African American waiter in Beller's novel explains, he was not about to spend "one solitary nickel" so he can "ogle a bunch of namby-pamby honky boys' wet dreams about 'how it gonna be'":

> Twenty, hundred, three hundred years make no difference to people like me and you. "The future," just a damn term, as in jail term, to keep things the way they is, somethin' to dangle in front of the likes of yours and mines so we shut up and start maybe believing our granchillrens will get a whack at somethin' better, that they gonna be able to live "with dignity and respect" in the future. But don't never forget the whole damn thing is orchestrated by that crew of crackers gettin' sentimental 'bout what they think their egg-and-sperm work gonna get 'em in the by-and-by. But for people like you and me, no matter *how* many exhibits, giveaways, promotions, and free things they got going out there, no matter how "fantastic" and "incredible" those dumb-assed white fools at them papers keep tellin' it, it don't mean shinola to people like you and me, not a single, solitary inch of it. (153-4)

As Beller, Doctorow, Groening, Womack, and Binder all demonstrate, the fair's utopian urban displays presented an elegant, streamlined façade of late-1930s America, but beneath that façade lurked a wide range of contradictory corporate, racist, and violent practices that the fair ignored and repressed. In true machine-age fashion, it just streamlined them away.

Like the World's Fair itself, contemporary historical and cultural representations of the fair explore the competing spatial paradigms that were established by the fair's utopian urban exhibits and alternative anti-modernist spaces, such as Dalí's Dream of Venus, that attempted to deconstruct the fair's urban ideology. The dynamics of this conflict can be seen in a series of confrontations between Dreyfus's Democracity and Dalí's Dream of Venus, between Gelernter's ride on the Futurama and Beller's, between Westinghouse's time capsule and Groening's or Doctorow's, and between Gelernter's nostalgic historical romance of the fair and Beller's postmodern meta-historical deconstruction of it. These kinds of socio-spatial conflicts not only permeated both the fair and its late-1930s historical context, but they also helped shape the historical evolution of post-WWII American urban space and culture. Consequently, the cultural debates that have emerged, both from the fair itself and from later attempts to either reconstruct or deconstruct the fair, represent a prototype of the cultural antagonisms that subsequently emerged in post-WWII New York City between International Style Modernist architects and urban planners on the one hand, and the writers, artists, and other intellectuals who opposed post-WWII American urbanism on the other hand. Understanding both the fair itself and conflicting interpretations of it, therefore, helps establish a historical and theoretical framework for analyzing the urban space and culture of post-WWII New York City.

Having completed our archaeological excavation of the pre-history of post-WWII New York City, let us now turn the page and step out of the "false, perfect World of Tomorrow fixed inside Futurama" onto the "real" intersections of post-WWII New York City (Beller 23). Now that we have witnessed the utopian projections of the past, all eyes to the brave new radiant—or was that homogeneous, federally subsidized, auto-centric, megalopolitan, corporate—cities of the future. But watch your step, and look out for speeding cars. (After all, both Jackson Pollock and Frank O'Hara, the most prominent artist and poet of the post-WWII New York avant-garde, were killed by them.) And be careful for the Cedar Bar, the cultural intersection where post-WWII New York City's artistic and literary avant-garde converged, debated, drank, and occasionally brawled. I don't want any of you to get caught in the crosstown traffic (and crossfire) between the city and its avant-garde. But it's time to get moving because the show's over. Everybody off the Streamline Express. The 1939–40 New York World's Fair is shutting down: it's slamming the doors on the past, locking them up, and throwing away the keys. Before we turn the last page on the fair, however, it is only appropriate that we give the Futurama the last word:

> Here you see a close-up view of one section of the great metropolis of 1960. The traffic system is the result of exhaustive surveys of the highway and street problems of the past. Modern efficient city planning—breath-taking architecture—each city block a complete unit in itself. Broad, one-way thoroughfares—space, sunshine, light and air. But here is an important intersection in the great metropolis of 1960! On the four corners are an Auditorium, a "Department Store," an "Apartment House" and an Automobile Display Salon. In a moment we will arrive actually on this very street intersection—to become a part of this self-same scene in the world of Tomorrow—in the wonder world of 1960—1940 is twenty years ago. ALL EYES TO THE FUTURE. (General Motors Corporation 19–20)

But watch your step as you exit the Futurama onto the "real" intersections of post-WWII New York City because the post-WWII New York avant-garde is going to have the last laugh.

Chapter Two

"Moloch whose skyscrapers stand in the long streets like endless Jehovahs!"

Deconstructing the Architexture of International Style Modernism

Moloch whose buildings are judgment! . . .
Moloch whose skyscrapers stand in the long streets like endless Jehovahs!
—Allen Ginsberg, from "Howl"

N O LONGER IMPEDED BY EITHER ECONOMIC DEPRESSION OR WAR, ARCHITECTS AND URBAN planners began radically reconstructing post-WWII New York City according to the geometrical architectural and urban paradigms developed at the 1939–40 New York World's Fair. As Robert A. M. Stern explains, it was:

International Style Modernism, first directly experienced by a broad American audience at the New York World's Fair of 1939–40, that would come to dominate postwar architecture in New York. Whereas Modern Classicism sought to marry traditional architecture and urbanistic conventions with a minimalist and machine-inspired aesthetic that seemed an appropriate expression of contemporary conditions, International Style Modernism sought to fully supersede old aesthetic systems and criteria . . . [and] transform all aesthetic and functional requirements into pure geometry. (*New York 1960*, 47)

Rows of International Style Modernist glass-and-steel-box skyscrapers and concrete-slab housing projects realized the essential spirit, if not the exact details, of Democracity's and Futurama's dense, techno-rational urban cores. Vast sprawling suburbs such as Levittown extended the city's periphery across a multi-state megalopolitan region that actualized the suburban ideals of Willard Van Dyke and Ralph Steiner's *The City*. The increasingly brutal functionalism of Robert Moses's postwar highways connected Manhattan with its expanding suburbs through a network of neo-Geddesian "magic" motorways. At the World's Fair, fairgoers previewed miniaturized models of these brave new urban spaces, but the city's postwar restructuring enabled New Yorkers to actually enter inside the fair's futuristic dream cities as a present-day reality. Despite the fair's "many erroneous predictions," David Gelernter argues that post-WWII America "realized the heart" of the fair's urban ideology: the "fair made promises that came true. It expressed hopes that have largely been fulfilled" (71, 34). By the Futurama's projected date of 1960, legislative landmarks such as the Housing Act of 1949, the Federal-Aid Highway Act of 1956, and the 1961 revision of New York City's zoning laws had established legal mechanisms and financial incentives that firmly entrenched the fair's urban ideology as the dominant paradigm of post-WWII American urbanism.

Many New Yorkers embraced these new urban practices, which they had eagerly anticipated since first previewing them at the World's Fair. By the end of the 1950s, "1.2 million whites moved out of the city, mostly to nearby suburban counties in New York and New Jersey" (Stern et al., *New York 1960*, 15). By the end of the 1960s, New York City had experienced a construction boom unprecedented in human history:

> Although the 7,806,000 square feet of new space in 1967 set a postwar record, the boom continued to pick up speed, with 8,820,000 square feet built in 1968, 10,187,000 square feet in 1969 and 14,280,000 square feet in 1970, which included the three million square feet of the World Trade Center. All in all, the amount built in this three year period not only represented half the total production of all the postwar years combined but was greater than that erected during the entire period of the city's post-World War I office building boom. (Stern et al., *New York 1960*, 64)

With International Style Modernist corporate skyscrapers accounting for most of this construction, widespread support for post-WWII New York City's new architectural and urban practices extended from the city's most powerful corporations to its average citizens. Yet, the New York cultural avant-garde almost unanimously opposed this spatial restructuring on both aesthetic and political grounds. What others saw as a brave, new utopian city—the rationalized, radiant, rectilinear city of tomorrow promised by the World's Fair—the avant-garde attacked as a brutal inscription of the political economy of post-WWII corporate America. For example, Norman Mailer criticized International Style Modernism's "lack of ornamentation, complexity, and mystery" as a "totalitarian" ideology that "beheads individuality, variety, dissent, extreme possibility, romantic faith; it blinds vision, deadens instinct; it obliterates the past" (97). Similarly, James Baldwin argued that Harlem's new hyper-functionalist, concrete-slab housing projects were:

> hated almost as much as policemen, and this is saying a great deal. And they are hated for the same reasons: both reveal, unbearably, the real attitude of the white world, no matter how many liberal speeches are made, no matter how many lofty

editorials are written, no matter how many civil-rights commissions are set up. (73)

Ferlinghetti also satirized the city's "surrealist landscape" of "supermarket suburbs" as the "shorn-up fragments / of the immigrant's dream come too true / and mislaid / among the sunbathers," while Ginsberg described the city's "robot apartments," "blind suburbs," and "sphinxes of cement and aluminum" as "Moloch the incomprehensible prison! Moloch the cross-bone soulless jailhouse and Congress of sorrows! Moloch whose buildings are judgment! Moloch the vast stone of war! Moloch the stunned governments!" (Ferlinghetti 13; Ginsberg 131). On virtually all fronts, the avant-garde aggressively opposed post-WWII New York City's homogeneous glass-and-steel box corporate skyscrapers, concrete-slab housing projects, ersatz suburbs, and proliferating commuter highways.

While it is not surprising that writers would criticize post-WWII American urbanism for its bland and boring aesthetics, the vitriolic passion of their diatribes suggested that they found something more problematic about this new urban ideology than its vulgar aesthetics. In addition to seeing the city's banal, repetitive "boxes made of ticky-tacky" as aesthetically insipid, they also criticized the city's new architectural and urban practices as part of a more ominous and ubiquitous socio-spatial regime that was pervasively transforming the topography of post-WWII America both aesthetically and politically. They criticized this new socio-spatial regime both for being aesthetically unimaginative and for being politically "totalitarian." Moreover, this rigid socio-spatial ideology not only inflicted various kinds of psycho-social damage on urban subjects, communities, and cultures, but it also menaced and threatened the American aesthetic imagination. It "destroyed" the "best mind's of [a] generation" and "ate up" their "imagination" (Ginsberg 126, 131). The New York avant-garde was not simply displeased with the city's postwar restructuring. It was actively preparing itself for an aggressive confrontation with the city's master builders on multiple political and aesthetic fronts.

Baited by these caustic attacks, the architectural and urban planning community jumped into the ring to challenge these cultural provacateurs, dismissing the avant-garde's urban critique as a tale full of sound and fury that signified nothing. Vincent Scully argued that "[a]way from words or the movies, an inability to cope with constructed reality seems to overwhelm the literati, and they tend to fall feebly back upon the simple narrative esthetic for the visual arts that they learned on their mother's knee," while Robert Moses contended that "few writers" knew "intimately the New York of today so as to be able to appraise it," and he criticized even the best writers for merely representing "only a quarter, a corner, phase or facet, certainly not the essence" of the city's totality (Scully 96; Moses 52).

Moreover, this dismissive view of post-WWII New York literature was broadly shared by many cultural critics. Post-WWII New York writers associated with the Beat Generation were repeatedly denounced as "bewildered internal cosmonauts" who advocated "prolonging adolescence to the grave," "know-nothing" bohemians with a "hostility to intelligence" and a "pathetic poverty of feeling," and anti-intellectuals who shunned "consciousness as if it were a plague" and wanted to create a literature "as absolute as the sun, as unarguable as orgasm, and as delicious as a lollipop" (Fiedler 399, 385; Prodhoretz 307, 315; Howe, "Mass Society," 436 and "The New York Intellectuals," 273). Amidst this barrage of attacks and counter-attacks, both sides specifically blamed each other for the dissolution of American cities. On the one hand, Norman Prodhoretz explained the postwar rise in juvenile crime "partly in terms of the same resentment against normal feeling and the attempt to cope with the world through intelligence that lies behind Kerouac and Ginsberg," whose "ethos shades off into violence and criminality, main-line drug addiction and madness" (318, 308). On the other hand, Baldwin blamed urban degeneration not on the rebellious cultural avant-garde, but rather on the racist contradictions and brutal functionalist aesthetics of International Style Modernist urbanism itself:

> The projects are hideous, of course, there being a law, apparently respected throughout the world, that popular housing shall be as cheerless as a prison. They are lumped all over Harlem, colorless, bleak, high, and revolting. . . . Harlem got its first private project, Riverton—which is now, naturally, a slum—about twelve years ago because at that time Negroes were not allowed to live in Stuyvesant Town. Harlem watched Riverton go up, therefore, in the most violent bitterness of spirit, and hated it long before the builders arrived. They began hating it about the time people began moving out of their condemned houses to make room for this additional proof of how thoroughly the white world despised them. And they had scarcely moved in, naturally, before they began smashing windows, defacing walls, urinating in the elevators, and fornicating in the playgrounds. Liberals, both black and white, were appalled at the spectacle. I was appalled by the liberal innocence—or cynicism, which comes out in practice as much the same thing. (73)

Both sides recognized that post-WWII New York City was beginning to explode into the urban crises of the 1960s, but the avant-garde blamed this urban decay on the internal contradictions of the master builders' flawed blueprints, while the architectural and urban planning community dismissed the avant-garde's urban critique as irrational, irrelevant, adolescent whining that promoted violence and criminality.

Cutting through the rhetorical smoke screens thrown up by both sides' hyperbolic recriminations, what really was at stake in this confrontation between the city's master builders and its cultural avant-garde? Was the avant-garde's urban critique nothing more than the misguided, idealism of "know-nothing bohemians" and "bewildered internal cosmonauts" who were unable to "cope with constructed reality?" Or did post-WWII New York writers' chaotic "sudden flash of the alchemy of the use of the ellipse the catalog the meter & the vibrating plane" somehow articulate a more sophisticated street-smart understanding of cities rooted in their own street-level urban experiences rather than the master builders' totalizing panoptic perspective (Ginsberg 130)? Was the cultural avant-garde's urban critique trapped within the myopic perspective of some merely local "corner" of the city, or did it explore a more comprehensive understanding of the city's vast, complex, heterogeneous geography? Was it merely a politically ineffective, or perhaps even reactionary, exercise in aesthetic experimentation, or did it perform some kind of material cultural work that had meaningful political and urban consequences? And why did this cultural confrontation focus so repeatedly on urban spaces as politically charged sites where the ideological conflicts of post-WWII America were palpably manifested and debated?

Moreover, why did this confrontation emerge at this particular historical moment? After all, one can at least historically contextualize why Herman Melville's "Bartleby, the Scrivener" and Henry James's *The American Scene* attacked New York City's bold skyscraper architecture when it was still shockingly new. It makes sense that urban subjects who were still adjusting to the skyscraper's unprecedented, inhuman immensity would find it alienating and oppressive. Working in the shadows of the city's early proto-skyscraper architecture, Bartleby's desk was placed in a recently dehumanized urban environment:

> close up to a small side-window in that part of the room, a window which origi-
> nally had afforded a lateral view of certain grimy back-yards and bricks, but which,
> owing to subsequent erections, commanded at present no view at all, though it
> gave some light. Within three feet of the panes was a wall, and the light came
> down from far above, between two lofty buildings, as from a very small opening
> in a dome. (9)

Deprived of space, light, air, and other elementary necessities by these "subsequent" architectural "erections," the colossal "Egyptian character of the [city's] masonry" crushed Bartleby both physically and psychologically (33). Returning to New York City after several years in Europe, James also described the city's new towering skyscrapers as a brutal expression of a "particular type of dauntless power":

> The aspect the power wears then is indescribable; it is the power of the most
> extravagant of cities, rejoicing, as with the voice of the morning, in its might, its
> fortune, its unsurpassable conditions, and imparting to every object and element,
> to the motion and expression of every floating, hurrying, panting thing, to the
> throb of ferries and tugs, to the plash of waves and the play of winds and the glint

of lights and the shrill of whistles and the quality and authority of breeze-borne cries—all, practically, a diffused, wasted clamour of *detonations*—something of its sharp free accent and, above all, of its sovereign sense of being "backed" and able to back. (59)

For James, however, these skyscrapers were "an expression of things lately and currently *done*," and consequently his complaint that their "huge, continuous fifty-floored conspiracy" had "amputated . . . half my history" at least makes historical sense as an expression of the shock of modernity (58, 71). Similarly, when Pietro di Donato's *Christ in Concrete* censured the corrupt and unstable foundations of New York City's post-WWI construction boom, it did so *post facto* from the historical perspective of the Great Depression. Di Donato's working-class, Italian-American immigrant novel described how the "bottom of [his characters'] world gave way" when the skyscraper that they were constructing suddenly "shuddered violently, her supports burst with the crackling slap of wooden gunfire," crushing them beneath "[w]alls, floors, beams [that] became whirling solid, splintering waves crashing with detonations that ground man and material in bonds of death" (14). But this thinly veiled allegory of the city's catastrophic economic crash expresses sentiments that are thoroughly grounded in their Depression-era historical context.

FROM INDUSTRIAL TO POSTINDUSTRIAL URBANISM

> Stone is now more stone than before.
> —Friedrich Nietzsche, from *Human, All Too Human*

The post-WWII New York avant-garde's diatribes against their city, however, reflected the evolving topography of a new epoch in American urban history. Even if International Style Modernist architecture did redress the city's skyline in a new rectilinear aesthetic, the inordinate immensity of skyscraper architecture per se no longer conveyed the shocking advent of modernity described by Melville and James. Similarly, the period's unprecedented economic boom seemed to provide little motivation for the discontentment voiced by di Donato. At the height of what Henry Luce has dubbed the "American Century," in the de facto international economic and cultural capital of this emerging epoch, New York City's cultural avant-garde turned against the city's master builders. It aggressively confronted the city's new urban ideology, an ideology that most New Yorkers had eagerly anticipated since they first caught a glimpse of it at the World's Fair. Yet in direct contrast with their contemporaries, the avant-garde attacked the socio-spatial regime of post-WWII American urbanism with the same critical intensity as Melville, James, and di Donato, albeit in dif-

ferent ways and for different reasons. They shared their predecessors' sense
of the city as a brutal expression of American culture's fusion of
Enlightenment techno-rationalism with a capitalist political economy, criticizing the city for having "blood" of "running money," a "mind" of "pure
machinery," and a "soul" of "electricity and banks" (Ginsberg 131). But
they did not describe this techno-fetishist corporate city as either shockingly new or apocalyptically self-imploding. Ginsberg's Moloch embodied
what James described as the "sovereign sense of being 'backed' and able to
back," but it was not an "expression of things lately and currently *done*"
(James 58–9). Like di Donato's collapsing skyscraper city, Ginsberg's
Moloch also "ground man and material in bonds of death"—its
"sphinx[es] of cement and aluminum bashed open their skulls and ate up
their imagination"—but it was not a city that had just collapsed or even a
city that teetered precariously on the verge of collapsing (di Donato 14;
Ginsberg 131). Rather, it was both "endless" and "invincible" (131). Like
the city of Enoch, it was eternal, omnipotent, and ethereal. It was a city
that could be lifted up to heavenly heights: "Pavements, trees, radios, tons!
lifting the city to Heaven which exists and is everywhere about us!" (132).
Like the shiny, sleek, glass-and-steel surfaces of International Style
Modernist corporate skyscrapers—which Hitchcock and Johnson defined
by their emphasis on volume or "space enclosed by thin planes or surfaces
as opposed to the suggestion of mass and solidity"—the city of Moloch
rose like a "spectral" apparition of "Light streaming out of the sky"
(Hitchcock and Johnson 13; Ginsberg 132, 131). It did not crush the
Bartleby-esque body of humanity beneath its oppressive "Egyptian . . .
masonry," so much as it destroyed the "minds" of its generation with more
rarified "cloud[s] of sexless hydrogen" that produced an immaterial sense
of "consciousness without a body" (131).

Ginsberg and other Post-WWII New York writers criticized the newly
emergent post-industrial city as violent and dehumanizing, but not quite in
the same way that Mellville, James, or di Donato represented the violence
of an earlier industrial city. Moloch was unnatural, but it did not impose a
massive industrial machinery upon the organic rhythms of nature—like
Eliot's *The Waste Land* with its "April is the cruelest month, breeding /
lilacs out of the dead land"—so much as it created "invisible suburbs"
where "[p]avements, trees, radios, [and] tons" could all be levitated to
heavenly heights (Eliot 32; Ginsberg 131–2). It was a city that both produced and was produced by information, service industries, financial spec-
ulations, and sleek, shiny, new synthetic substances that had more volume
than mass. It was not without its industrial "filth" and "machinery," but it
was also, and perhaps even primarily, a "Mental Moloch," a city whose
"name is the Mind" (131). It was a city crowned with both "smokestacks
and antennae;" it was a city of both "demonic industries" and "skeleton

treasuries" (131–2). It was a city that needed to be "shivered" not to the
foundation of its factories but "down to the last radio" (131). This constant shifting in Ginsberg's rhetoric—both between industrial and postindustrial urban forms, and between material and immaterial images—
reflects how the socio-spatial topography of post-WWII New York City
was rapidly changing from an industrial urbanscape to what Arjun
Appadurai has described as a mediascape, or perhaps even what Foucault
describes as an epistemological "table, a *tabula*, that enables thought to
operate upon the entities of our world, to put them in order, to divide them
into classes, to group them according to names that designate their similarities and their differences—the table upon which, since the beginning of
time, language has intersected space" (*The Order of Things*, xvii).

Ginsberg's "Howl" drew a line in the sand between the Molochian
techno-rational construction of the postindustrial corporate American city
on the one hand, and the cultural architectonics of a counter-hegemonic
new American poetics on the other. It described the newly emerging urban
topography of post-WWII America, but it depicted that topography in
terms that reflected the postindustrialization of global capitalism, the
United States' geopolitical dominance as a new international superpower,
and the way that these economic and geopolitical transitions were transforming post-WWII America's increasingly intertwined urbanscape-medi-
ascapes. Postindustrial capitalism's increasing investments in information
technologies such as film, radio, television, and computers might not have
inscribed themselves as noticeably onto the city's material urban skyline,
but they had a dramatic and pervasive impact on the lives of urban subjects, creating new cultural and political possibilities and establishing new
kinds of urban spaces, subjectivities, and communities. That Ginsberg
located the principal thrust of his urban critique not in some kind of material urban politics, but rather in the semiotic deconstruction of the architectonics of language itself—in his attempt to "recreate the syntax and
measure of poor human prose"—demonstrates his prophetic perceptive-
ness to how the postindustrial postmodernization of the capitalist economy
was transforming post-WWII American urban and cultural practices (130).
In addition, this postindustrial transformation of economic and urban
processes helps explain why Ginsberg and other post-WWII cultural producers turned so frequently to the complex, heterogeneous topography of
marginalized urban spaces as a primary model for their own counter-hegemonic political and experimental practices.

First, the post-WWII New York avant-garde explored marginal urban
spaces because they reflected and revealed the contradictory and fragmented geography of postindustrial capitalism, while the dominant socio-spatial
regime of post-WWII American urbanism attempted to conceal and mask
these contradictions beneath its smooth, shiny, homogeneous, geometrical

aesthetics. Even without politically agitating for material urban reforms, the avant-garde's critical analysis of urban space often functioned, on an allegorical or metaphorical level, as a politically engaged critique of post-WWII corporate capitalism. In particular, works such as "Howl," George Oppen's "Tourist Eye," Donald Barthelme's "The Glass Mountain," and Ernesto Cardenal's "Room 5600" used ambiguous, negative, and fragmented representations of skyscrapers to deconstruct the skyscraper's—and hence corporate America's—traditional function as the socio-spatial center of American cities.

In addition, post-WWII New York writers such as Ginsberg, O'Hara, and Jack Micheline turned to the complex, heterogeneous topography of industrial cityscapes in order to shore up psycho-social subjectivities threatened by postindustrial processes that increasingly imposed new media- and info-scapes on top of an anterior industrial city. Much like Melville, James, Eliot, di Donato, and other modernists who turned back to the socio-spatial topography of previous agrarian landscapes to shore up subjectivities threatened by industrialization and urbanization, the post-WWII New York avant-garde turned to complex, heterogeneous urban spaces themselves as a bulwark against postindustrialization. Only now, the material evolution of capitalism had begun shifting toward a new stage, so instead of looking back from industrial cityscapes to agrarian landscapes, the post-WWII New York avant-garde turned back from newly emerging postindustrial media- and info-scapes to the now "pastoralized" industrial cityscape itself. As postindustrialization transformed city life into a kind of second nature, nature proper retreated further into a pre-historical, quasi-mythic past. This helps explain why writers such as Ginsberg and O'Hara frequently fused and confused urban and pastoral imagery because they increasingly used the materiality of urban images as a kind of "urban-pastoral" defense against the postindustrial dematerialization of urban space. To exorcise these postindustrial demons that were eating up their "brains and imagination" and turning them into "consciousness[es] without a body," the post-WWII New York avant-garde associated their aesthetic and political resistance with marginal urban spaces where they "sank all night in submarine light of Bickford's" in Times Square or "sat through the stale beer afternoon in desolate Fugazi's" in Greenwich Village (Ginsberg 131, 126). For Nietzsche, industrialization had made stone "more stone than before" (quoted in Buddensieg 5). By destroying the natural world of stone and making it more scarce, industrialization made stone more vividly present to the Romantic aesthetic imagination. Similarly, by making complex, heterogeneous urban spaces themselves more scarce, the postindustrial restructuring of American cities endowed urban spaces with a new auratic intensity, making them more urban than before. As the "spectral" city of "Mental Moloch" was lifted into a postindustrial "Heaven which exists and is everywhere about us," post-WWII New York writers turned to the city's "tenement roofs," "unshaven rooms," "incomparable blind streets," "stoops off fire escapes," "Turkish bath[s]," and other marginal "gaps in Time & Space" as sites of sublime aesthetic rapture (126–32). In this new postindustrial context, the New York avant-garde increasingly turned to these marginal urban spaces as new frontiers for a free poetic life and new hinterlands for the aesthetic imagination.

DECONSTRUCTING THE INTERNATIONAL STYLE MODERNIST CORPORATE SKYSCRAPER: GEORGE OPPEN'S CRITIQUE OF LEVER HOUSE

The land

Lacked center:
We must look to Lever Brothers . . .

Why are the office

Buildings, storehouses of papers,
The centers of extravagance?

—George Oppen, from "Tourist Eye"

Writing both within and against this postindustrial urban context, the post-WWII New York avant-garde developed new aesthetic strategies for representing, analyzing, and imagining alternatives to the spatial restructuring of American cities. In particular, they attempted to demonstrate how International Style Modernist architecture and urban planning functioned as both a symbolic mirror and an ideological mask by simultaneously revealing and concealing the cultural logic of post-WWII corporate capitalism. As a symbolic expression of the material culture that produced it, International Style Modernism's bland, homogeneous, geometrical spatial aesthetics materially inscribed the ideology of post-WWII corporate America onto the urban and architectural spaces of New York City. Unlike the rugged individualism of 1920s entrepreneurial capitalism, post-WWII corporate America promoted what William H. Whyte, Jr. described as a "collectivization" that forced people to adapt to the post-WWII restructuring of the capitalist political economy by accepting "'belongingness' as the ultimate need of the individual" and "sublimating [themselves] in the group" (4, 7–8). While it is true that some people resisted this psychosocial adjustment to corporate culture, the majority conformed, and as they did so they became all the more receptive to the "pure geometry" of post-WWII American urbanism. As Whyte explained, post-WWII America's homogeneous suburbs functioned as "the dormitory of the new generation of organization men" because both shared a common cultural logic that subordinated individual self-expression to the homogeneous socio-spatial cohesion of the collective (10). Similarly, Stern et al. have interpreted International Style Modernist architecture as another manifestation of this same social transformation:

> By the late 1940s, as the swaggering individual entrepreneur of the past was transformed into the team-playing corporate man in the gray flannel suit, so the instantly identifiable cathedrals of commerce that exemplified the city's architecture from 1900 to 1929 gave way to an architecture that celebrated repetition to the point of anonymity. (*New York 1960*, 47)

International Style Modernism's "nearly identical," "anonymously detailed," and "blandly profiled" glass-and-steel boxes embodied the corporate ideologies described by such classic works of post-WWII American sociology as William H. Whyte, Jr.'s *The Organization Man*, C. Wright Mills's *White Collar*, and David Riesman and Nathan Glazer's *The Lonely Crowd*—or represented in novels of corporate angst such as Sloan Wilson's *The Man in the Gray Flannel Suit* (Stern et al., *New York 1960*, 47, 53). For example, International Style Modernism's rejection of "arbitrary applied decoration" resembled the self-effacing fashion of Sloan's man in the gray flannel suit because both celebrated the corporate values of homogeneity and sobriety (Hitchcock and Johnson 20). The anti-individualistic aesthetic of Mies van der Rohe's Seagram Building, which Mies himself described as "completely opposed to the idea that a specific building should have an individual character," expressed the same anonymity as Whyte's "organization man," who assumes the "vows of organization life" and "rationalizes the organization's demands for fealty" by converting "what would seem in other times a bill of no rights into a restatement of individualism" (Mies, quoted in Stern et al., *New York 1960*, 344; Whyte 3, 6). Because of this anti-individualistic, bland, anonymous, homogeneous aesthetic, International Style Modernist corporate architecture both materially embodied and symbolically expressed the emerging ideology of post-WWII corporate capitalism.

Critical of the socio-political implications of these radically homogeneous spatial practices, the post-WWII New York avant-garde attempted to deconstruct the socio-spatial ideology of International Style Modernist corporate architecture. For example, George Oppen's "Tourist Eye" decenters corporate architecture's traditional function as the privileged center, the urban core, around which urban topographies were organized. In the poem's first section, Oppen openly questions whether International Style Modernist corporate "office / Buildings, storehouses of paper" could provide a "final meaning" for the modern urban experience (*Collected Poems*, 43). Oppen specifically asks why we "must look to Lever Brothers" to provide the missing "center" that the city "lacked" (43).

As Oppen's imagery suggests, Lever House cannot center the city's urban topography because it is merely a local address: it only covers a single "square block," containing some "thousand lives / Within that glass" (43). Reversing the dismissive arguments used against the Beat Generation, Oppen's images suggest that Lever House itself was merely one provincial part of the city. It could not stand, like a spatial synecdoche, for the urban whole any more than Ginsberg's "negro streets" or O'Hara's "lunch hour" walks could. Turning away from Lever House's "lights that blaze and promise," other sections of the poem explore alternative urban spaces: the "most worn places / Where chance moved among the crowd," the "aging homes / Of the workmen," the "red buildings of Red Hook," and the "Brooklyn Hardware stores" (43–5). In particular, Oppen finds in these alternative urban spaces a "sense of order," an "essential city," and a "necessary city" that "among these harbor streets [is] still visible" (45). Inverting the center-margin, order-chaos, necessary-arbitrary dichotomies that structured International Style Modernism's socio-spatial ideology, "Tourist Eye" challenges the spatial restructuring of post-WWII New York City. If a "sense of order" is "still visible" within the city's "most worn spaces," and even Lever House's "pure geometry" cannot provide the city with the "center" that it "lacked," then International Style Modernist architecture cannot provide post-WWII American cities with either an aesthetic or a political panacea. Beneath its geometrical facades, it might even harbor irrational and violent forces that could disrupt some alternative "essential" or "necessary" "sense of order" that is "still visible" in marginal urban spaces.

Like Ginsberg's "Howl," the larger significance of Oppen's poetry is found not only in its overt critique of International Style Modernism but also in the covert "architextural" relationships that it explores between its alternative sense of urban space and its experimental aesthetic practices. While Oppen's work never reaches the same chaotic, frenetic pitch sounded by "Howl," Marjorie Perloff has argued that it is "more disjointed" than William Carlos Williams' poetry: "If Williams' is a metric of action, the creation of a field of force in which the presence of the moment is made manifest, Oppen's 'discrete series' of lines remains disjunctive, discriminatory, abrupt—a movement of fits and starts" (123, 132). In "Tourist Eye," Oppen uses such disjunctive textual structures specifically to express his alternative sense of urban space, as the following lines demonstrate:

The lights that blaze and promise
Where are so many—What is offered

In the wall and nest of lights?
The land

Lacked center:
We must look to Lever Brothers

based in a square block,
A thousand lives

Within that glass. What is the final meaning
Of extravagance? Why are the office

Buildings, storehouses of papers,
The centers of extravagance?
                    (43. Used by Permission of New Directions Publishing Corporation)

While these lines seemingly present a straightforward attack on the axiological centrality of International Style Modernist architecture, the rhetorical force of that attack is born by their complex, heterogeneous textual
structure as much as it is by the words' semantic denotations. By juxtaposing the missing urban "center" with Lever House's "square block" at
the end of two lines, the poem rhetorically emphasizes how International
Style Modernism's orthogonal geometry can not fill the city's need for a less
linear kind of urban order. International Style Modernism's architectural
square pegs don't quite fit the city's round urban holes. This tension is further emphasized by the opposition between the words "lacked" and
"based" that begin these two lines. These conflicting images suggest the
poem's uncertainty about whether the city's center is "based" upon some
solid ground or suspended above some foundationless "lack." By juxtaposing "Lever Brothers" and "thousand lives" at the end of the two lines
following these conflicting images, the poem suggests that a similar fissure
might exist between the corporation and its employees. On the one hand,
the poem splits the phrase "final meaning / Of extravagance" across two
lines in order to reinforce syntactically the grammatical ambiguity between
the "final meaning" that it seeks and the "extravagance" that it finds. On
the other hand, Oppen conjoins the phrases "Buildings, storehouses of
papers" to syntactically reinforce, the ambiguity between the material
solidity of the city's architectural "buildings" and the abstract ephemerali-
ty of its economic activities, the "papers" that are produced and stored
inside these material buildings. Constantly oscillating between these incon-
gruous juxtapositions and syntactic discontinuities, Oppen's poetry creates
a complex tension between its search for a final, centered, grounded
order—whether urban or textual—and its critical deconstruction of such

totalizing orders. This disjointed textual structure resembles Arjun Appadurai's description of how the "complex, overlapping, disjunctive order" of global capitalism simultaneously homogenizes and heterogenizes global cultural and political practices (32). In addition, the poem further interrogates International Style Modernist architecture by only referring once to the city's architectural "office / Buildings" themselves while repeatedly evoking their various aesthetic, economic, and political functions. It refers to the corporation, "Lever Brothers," that uses the building, instead of the building, Lever House, itself. It also describes the city's International Style Modernist architecture in terms of its "glass" aesthetics, "square block" real estate investments, and economic functions as "storehouses of papers" produced by the "thousand lives" who work "Within that glass." By connecting International Style Modernist architecture to what Appadurai describes as the heterogeneous "dimensions of global cultural flows," this multi-faceted depiction of Lever House demonstrates how International Style Modernism's socio-spatial ideology fuses a wide range of overlapping, yet disjunctive, aesthetic, economic, and political systems (33). Instead of bifurcating its exploration of order and fragmentation into two diametrically opposed urban and textual structures, as Ginsberg's "Howl" does, "Tourist Eye" superimposes them on top of each other to create a complex, heterogeneous "architexturality" that oscillates between its centripetal quest for structural order and its centrifugal exploration of alternative, complex, heterogeneous orders. Moreover, the push and pull of these competing forces is profoundly shaped by Oppen's simultaneous engagement with various architectural, urban, and textual structures.

The complex "architexturality" of Oppen's poetry is brilliantly illustrated both by its description of Lever House as a "wall and nest of lights" and by its description of International Style Modernist corporate skyscrapers as "centers of extravagance." As these ambiguous phrases suggest, International Style corporate architecture cannot be reduced solely to a series of radically homogeneous, rigid, orthogonal "walls" both anchored to and anchored by urban "centers." In addition, it also functioned as a centrifugal avian "nest" from which the fledgling processes of global capitalism took off in "extravagan[t]" postindustrial, transnational flights. It was a socio-spatial launching pad for the far-reaching global exchanges of transnational corporations such as Lever Brothers. It was also an ethereal postindustrial machine—not for living in but for producing "storehouses of paper," the principal product of the postindustrial economy. In this sense, the "pure geometry" of International Style Modernist architecture functioned more like a mask than a mirror. It dissembled these extravagant, deterritorialized—both postnational and postindustrial—flights by covering them over with a rigid, geometrical aesthetic facade.

If one can look past the dissembling "walls" of Lever House's "pure geometry," however, one can still discern architectural traces of how it symbolically expressed postindustrial, transnational capitalism's deterritorialized and deterritorializing "extravagance." At the same time that its gridded exterior and glass-and-steel box structure finally realized the "thirty-year-old utopistic ideas of Mies van der Rohe and Le Corbusier . . . at full scale," its primary building slab was also "lifted on a base and turned at a right angle to the grand axis of Park Avenue, the traditional street— the *rue corridor* so loathed by Le Corbusier" to create a "new urban order of individual, objectlike buildings 'liberated' in space and set apart from one another" (Stern et al., *New York 1960*, 338–9). With this radical, deterritorializing gesture, Lever House revealed the contradictory, heterogeneous, and anti-urban nature of post-WWII American urbanism. While Lever House itself was radically homogeneous, its anti-urban orientation perpendicular to the "grand axis of Park Avenue" established a stark dichotomy between its own "individual, objectlike" homogeneous space and the heterogeneous socio-spatial topography of the rest of the city. With this Janus-faced homogeneous-heterogeneous ambivalence, Lever House revealed traces of the contradictory violence that lurked beneath International Style Modernism's homogeneous, democratic urban facades. Lever House achieved its illusory "pure geometry" by deterritorializing itself from and turning its back to the complex, heterogeneous topography that shaped the rest of the city. Just as Jacobs has critiqued International Style Modernism's "dishonest mask of pretended order, achieved by ignoring or suppressing the real order that is struggling to exist and to be served," Lefebvre has also censured International Style Modernism's "pure geometry" because its so-called "'logic of space', with its apparent significance and coherence, actually conceals the violence inherent in abstraction," and consequently its radically homogeneous space "has nothing homogeneous about it. After its fashion, which is polyscopic and plural, it subsumes and unites scattered fragments or elements by force" (Jacobs 15; Lefebvre 306, 308). Deconstructing International Style Modernism's contradictory, violent, ambivalent socio-spatial logic, Oppen's "Tourist Eye" critically analyzes how urban "centers of extravagance" displace alternative "sense[s] of order" that are "still visible" in marginal urban spaces. Like a shifting holographic double-image, the irreducible ambivalence that pervades both Oppen's representations of architectural and urban spaces and his complex images and textual structures attempts to articulate how the centripetal-centrifugal, homogeneous-heterogeneous, push and pull of the emerging postindustrial economy shaped both the spatial and cultural practices of post-WWII New York City.

Chapter Three

The "eli eli lamma lamma sabacthani saxophone cry that shivered the cities"

The Liquid Geometries of Post-WWII Jazz Literature

> The singer, stamping her foot three times, led off into a fresh burst of song, rais-
> ing her arms in graceful supplication. "All of me-ee-ee . . . Why . . . not . . . take
> . . . all of me-ee-ee!" . . . Her dusky eyes leveled knowingly at each customer and,
> as though each saw there and heard in the music the memory they all must have
> attached to this rebellious and wistful American jazz which was somehow most
> expressive of the boiling, deaf cities . . .
>
> —John Clellon Holmes, from *Go*

AT SOME POINT OR ANOTHER, VIRTUALLY EVERY MAJOR POST-WWII JAZZ WRITER
explicitly associates jazz with space either by using spatial images to
represent jazz or by identifying jazz with some specific kind of space
or spatial sensibility. When the narrator of Ralph Ellison's *Invisible Man*
listens to Louis Armstrong's "What Did I Do to Be so Black and Blue," he
hears it "not only in time, but in space as well," and then he "descend[s],
like Dante, into its depths. And *beneath the swiftness of the hot tempo
there was a slower tempo and a cave and I entered it . . . and below that I
found a lower level and a more rapid tempo*" (9). Not only does Ellison
explicitly spatialize Armstrong's music, but he also describes it as opening
up suggestive subterranean psychological spaces. Bob Kaufman's poetry
also both depicts various kinds of jazz spaces—such as "yardbird corners,"
"pockets of joy, / And jazz," and "that Jazz corner of life" (*Cranial Guitar*,
92, 124, 102)—and uses spatial images to represent jazz. For example,
"On" describes Charlie Parker's music as "flights to sound filled pockets in
space," while "Walking Parker Home" portrays it as "boppy new ground,"
"bop mountains," and "pyramids of notes spontaneously exploding"
(*Cranial Guitar*, 92, 102). Jack Kerouac's *On the Road* also describes the
performance of a "wild tenorman bawling" as moving "up, down, side-
ways, upside down, horizontal, thirty degrees, forty degrees" (197, 199).
Several other post-WWII writers represent jazz using similar spatial images,

ranging from a "style with lots of space," "liquid geometry," and "architectural Miles Davis logics" to "cubist and surrealist patterns," "multi-colored n-dimension shadings," and *smashing all known dimensions /* Hurtling thru spacelanes of jazz" (Joans, *All of Ted Joans and No More*, 27; Hull 87; Kerouac 240–1; Kaufman, *Cranial Guitar*, 145; Stone 194; Troupe 37). Taken collectively, these recurring spatializations of jazz demonstrate how many post-WWII jazz writers perceived various kinds of interrelationships between jazz and space.

But why did these writers spatialize jazz? On what grounds did they base their associations between jazz and space? What exactly is the "architectural logic" of a Miles Davis solo or the "liquid geometry" of a Charlie Parker improvisation, and what kind of spaces are "Jazz corner[s]," "bop mountains," and "spacelanes of jazz"? Moreover, what kind of rhetorical and cultural work do these spatializations of jazz perform? After all, there is nothing obviously spatial about jazz: not only is jazz not spatial in any literal sense, but even metaphorical associations between jazz and space seem potentially problematic. When Ellison's Invisible Man hears Armstrong's music in "space" and descends "beneath" its tempo, he seems to confuse distinct sensory perceptions, and even Ted Joans's more plausible description of a jazz "style with lots of space" uses rhetorical sleight-of-hand to substitute vacant spaces for audible silences. By reasonably approximating the moods, rhythms, harmonies, and melodic structures of modern jazz, these spatial images do simplify the task of representing musical sounds in a non-musical linguistic medium, but is there a deeper sense in which these images function as more than interdisciplinary metaphors? Is there some more substantial reason for spatializing jazz, and what kind of rhetorical, cultural, and political work does this literary spatialization of jazz perform?

While readers might easily dismiss these spatializations of jazz as simply exercises in metaphor, or perhaps even catachresis, these recurring images suggest that post-WWII jazz writers found more significant, intrinsic relationships between jazz and space. In particular, many writers used spatial images of jazz to promote a specific conception of jazz as a radical cultural, political, epistemological, or existential paradigm shift. For example, Arthur Brown's "The Assassination of Charlie Parker" portrays Parker's music as "bluing a new cartography of flight / at the ear's horizon's deepest touch" (20), while Lynda Hull's "Orinthology" describes how Parker's "liquid geometry weaves *a way of thinking*, / a way of breaking / synchronistic / through time" (87). Both poems use spatialized images of jazz to associate Parker's music with new epistemologies of perception and understanding. Gilbert Sorrentino's *Steelwork* also uses spatial imagery to represent how two post-WWII American adolescents experience intense cognitive dissonance after hearing Parker's "KoKo" for the first time:

What did that mean? Gibby and Donnie G sat listening to it for the fourth time in Donnie's room. Whole pieces of their world were being chipped off and shredded, ruthlessly. Great blasts of foreign air. A foreign air, the whole wide world entering the house. . . . They were almost frightened. . . . They went outside and the street seemed different, they saw it narrow. With people closed out from the gigantic world. It had blasted a hole in the wall around them. (3)

Similarly, the complex stream-of-consciousness associations in Kaufman's "Does the Secret Mind Whisper?" also use spatial references to represent the revolutionary nature of Parker's music. Embedded within a long genealogical list, Kaufman includes the following series: "who begat picasso who begat charlie parker who begat morpheus" (*Cranial Guitar*, 147–48). This series associates jazz with other visual, spatial, and poetic revolutions by situating Parker between Picasso, whose iconoclastic art has become synonymous with modernist painting's radical visual experimentation, and "morpheus," a neologism that combines the Greek root for shape, "morph," with the name of the mythical Greek poet Orpheus, thereby suggesting an interrelationship between spatial and poetic forms. In isolation, Kaufman's imagery might seem arbitrary, but when viewed within the larger context of post-WWII jazz literature its associative logic corroborates other writers' sense that bebop jazz "expresses another mode of being. Another way of living. Another way of perceiving reality" (Baraka, *Autobiography*, 60). In post-WWII American jazz literature, spatialized images of jazz played a crucial role in representing and promoting such alternative modes of perceiving, imagining, and being.

Moreover, many post-WWII jazz writers specifically associated this counter-hegemonic jazz "structure of feeling" with particular kinds of urban spaces. Writers such as John Clellon Holmes, Allen Ginsberg, Bob Kaufman, Amiri Baraka, Sonia Sanchez, and Haki Madhubuti used jazz as one of their primary means of representing, analyzing, and imagining alternatives to the post-WWII restructuring of American cities. For example, Holmes's early Beat novel, *Go* (1952), describes jazz as "somehow most expressive of the boiling, deaf cities," and he repeatedly associates jazz with the Beat Generation's emerging urban subjectivity (138). His novel's primary metaphor for the Beat Generation derives from Hart Kennedy (Neal Cassady) responding to jazz performances by yelling "Go! Go!," and he describes "modern jazz" as providing the Beat Generation with "a gospel for the first time. It was more than a music; it became an attitude toward life, a way of walking, a language and a costume; and these introverted kids . . . who had never belonged anywhere before, now felt somewhere at last" (115, 161). Micheline also represents jazz as a quintessential expression of urban experience. In the poem, "Let's Ride on the Angel Goodbye," he depicts a character named Rainy who cannot get jazz out of his head when he walks around the city: he "always heard the cornet blowing. . . . Always at night he walked the streets alone, always the horn in his ears" (*North of Manhattan*, 58). In "Poet of the Streets," he describes a poet who discovers "something deeper than the stone cities . . . something deeper than our existence": "jazz horns and drummers / above concrete / above whimpering voices / above calculators" (*North of Manhattan*, 87). Time and time again, post-WWII writers represented jazz as an indispensable component of their urban experiences, and nowhere is this relationship between jazz and cities more evident than in the urban literature of post-WWII New York City—a literature pervaded with representations of jazz sounds, jazz rhythms, jazz performances, jazz clubs, jazz musicians, jazz spaces, jazz narratives, and jazz revolutions. Like the soundtrack in John Cassavetes's *Shadows*, jazz music provided a constant backdrop for post-WWII New York writers' explorations of their city.

In particular, many of these writers represented jazz specifically as a kind of oppositional urban discourse that both critiqued the dominant spatial logic of post-WWII American cities and enabled the exploration of alternative urban possibilities. In "Howl," for example, Ginsberg represents jazz as an apocalyptic-messianic "eli eli lamma lamma sabacthani saxophone cry that shivered the cities down to the last radio" (131), while Kaufman's poetry repeatedly describes jazz as an "unmistakable call to arms," "battle cries," or "windy saxophone revolutions" that "Swing higher / Defiantly into a challenge key" (*Cranial Guitar*, 145, 102, 63). In "Battle Report," Kaufman even more explicitly represents jazz as a military assault of one "thousand saxophones infiltrat[ing] the city":

> Five generals, gathered in the gallery,
> Blowing plans.
> At last, the secret code is flashed:
> Now is the time, now is the time.
> Attack: the sound of jazz.
> The City Falls. (110)

In addition to describing jazz as an oppositional force directed against the mainstream city, many writers also associate jazz with alternative counter-hegemonic urban paradigms. Turning away from the city's "skyscraping office buildings," Kaufman's "J'Accuse" explores the city's less sober and more passionate "vacant lots" and obscure "doorways we need, / to dig into each other's mouth and hair" (*Cranial Guitar*, 156). In other poems, Kaufman describes these alternative urban spaces as "Jazz corner[s] of Life" or "yardbird corners" where the "Jazz-tinted dawn" invites the "nerveless to feel once more / That fierce dying of humans consumed / In raging fires of Love" (*Cranial Guitar*, 92, 102). With these passionate images, Kaufman depicts how jazz expresses the kinds of emotions that post-WWII square America repressed. Similarly, Ginsberg's "Howl" describes the "best minds" of his generation dragging themselves "through the negro streets at dawn" and floating "across the tops of cities contemplating jazz" until they experience an "eli eli lamma lamma sabacthani saxophone cry that shivered the cities" (126, 131). Like Kaufman, Ginsberg also associates jazz with ecstatic modes of being and visionary kinds of perception and understanding that directly oppose the techno-rational, functionalist ideology of post-WWII urban redevelopment. Turning to jazz specifically to critique the socio-spatial restructuring of post-WWII American cities, many writers either represented jazz as a counter-hegemonic force that "shivered," "infiltrate[d]," and "attack[ed]" the city, or they described marginal jazz spaces that existed outside—at "*a lower level and a more rapid tempo*" than or "drift[ing] above"—the dominant socio-spatial logic of post-WWII American urbanism (Ginsberg 131; Kaufman, "Battle Report," 110; Ellison 9; Neal 145).

But why did these writers turn specifically to jazz in order to critique post-WWII urbanism and imagine utopic urban alternatives? What exactly did they find wrong with post-WWII American cities, and how did jazz represent some kind of alternative revolutionary urban paradigm? Moreover, why did this sense of jazz emerge primarily during a particular historical period in jazz literature—between the publication of Ellison's *Invisible Man* and Homles's *Go* in 1952 and the decline of the Black Arts Movement in the 1970s—which, in turn, corresponded to a specific moment in the evolution of American urban history: post-WWII corporate America's "near-total repudiation of traditional architecture in favor of International Style Modernism" and the consequent neo-Corbusian restructuring of post-WWII New York City between the completion of Gordon Bunshaft's/Skidmore, Owings, & Merrill's Lever House in 1952 and the completion of Minoru Yamasaki's/Emery Roth & Sons' World Trade Center in 1977 (Stern et al., *New York 1960*, 332)? In order to understand why so many writers embraced jazz as some kind of counter-hegemonic urban paradigm at this particular historical moment, one must both contextualize post-WWII jazz literature within the historical context of American urban history and critically analyze the socio-political significance of the spatial practices that defined the dominant trends in post-WWII American urbanism.

As Henri Lefebvre argues in *The Production of Space*, "every society—and hence every mode of production with its subvariants . . . produces a space, its own space," and consequently "the shift from one mode [of production] to another must entail the production of a new space" (31, 46). Because of its international importance as the de facto economic and cultural capital of post-WWII America, New York City became one of the principal locations where the "great age of the American corporation" produced one of its most distinctive spaces: the "glass-and-metal Modernist high rise," which soon became one of corporate America's "principal representations, just as the gray flannel suit became its sartorial signature" (Stern et al., *New York 1960*, 52). Applying a neo-Corbusian "pure geometry" to every aspect of skyscraper construction, International Style Modernist architects systematically restructured the spatial logic of New York City's prewar skyscraper architecture. Since the construction of New York City's first skyscraper, Daniel Burnham's 22–story Flatiron (Fuller) Building in 1902, New York architects have constructed ever-taller skyscrapers to create a skyline dramatically oriented toward an aesthetic of vertical extension. In addition, the landmark zoning law of 1916, which was pragmatically motivated to improve urban living conditions, had the unintended consequence of regulating the city's architectural aesthetics by mandating that all skyscrapers be structured according to a series of "wedding-cake" style architectural setbacks. While this zoning ordinance allowed significant architectural freedom to design diverse setback schemes, it set strict limits regarding how far skyscrapers could rise before they had to set themselves back from the street wall in order to allow more light and air to reach the city streets below. New York City's Beaux-Arts and Art Deco traditions further embellished the city's skyscrapers with both ornamental exterior decorations and elaborate ornamental spires.

Reversing these architectural precedents, International Style Modernist architects and urban planners reconstructed post-WWII New York City according to new modernist spatial practices. Beginning in 1947 with the Tishman Building, Park Avenue's first post-WWII office building, architectural firms such as Kahn & Jacobs began stripping traditional "prewar setback or 'wedding cake'" architectural structures of their exterior ornamentation and redressing them in the "new minimalist aesthetics of the International Style" by "alternating continuous bands of limestone and glass" and "fixed and double-hung windows" to create gridded exterior surfaces (Stern et al., *New York 1960*, 333). This pattern of redressing setback structures in the International Style's geometrical aesthetic was quickly replicated throughout post-WWII New York, especially by Emery Roth & Sons, in buildings such as their 505 Park Avenue and Colgate-Palmolive Building. It was the completion of Lever House in 1952, however, that most dramatically "announced the transformation of the aesthetics of American corporate architecture" by applying Le Corbusier's "pure geometry" not only to its exterior surface but also to its architectural structure (Stern et al., *New York 1960*, 338). In addition to replacing traditional decorative Beaux Arts exteriors with grided geometric surfaces, Lever House fulfilled the "thirty-year-old utopistic ideas of Mies van der Rohe and Le Corbusier" by flattening out New York City's traditional setback structures and ornamental spires into a flat-topped glass-and-steel box structure (Stern et al., *New York 1960*, 338). By 1958, Mies's own architectural masterpiece, the Seagram Building, clearly established International Style Modernism as *the* definitive style of post-WWII New York architecture. Even the ever-escalating vertical orientation that motivated New York architects for over half a century was replaced by International Style Modernism's obsession with geometrical grided exteriors and glass-and-steel box structures, since no new height record was set between the Empire State Building in 1930 and the World Trade Center in 1977—despite the tremendous post-WWII construction boom.

In and of itself, as merely a formal aesthetic style, International Style Modernism's neo-Corbusian geometry obviously offended more baroque sensibilities, but did it really warrant the diatribes directed against it by post-WWII jazz writers such as Joans, Kaufman, and Ginsberg who respectively described skyscrapers as "tombstones," "jealous bitch[es]," and "granite cocks" (Joans, *A Black Manifesto in Jazz Poetry and Prose*, 76; Kaufman, *Cranial Guitar*, 156; Ginsberg 132)? Moreover, did this "pure geometry" merit the equally fanatical praise of its advocates who often bankrolled it at an appreciable financial loss? After all, New York City's earliest International Style skyscrapers, such as Lever House (1952) and the Seagram Building (1958), were built before the 1961 revision of the city's zoning laws, and consequently the prevailing 1916 zoning laws prohibited their box-like structures from fully developing the economic potential of the sites where they were constructed. The corporations that financed these projects essentially assumed the financial losses created by not fully developing their property, and the city even taxed these unused spaces by assessing property values based on a property's potential rather than its actual leasable dimensions. The impassioned positions taken by both sides in the debates over post-WWII corporate architecture, therefore, suggest that International Style Modernism's architectural aesthetic performed some cultural work beyond mere aesthetic decoration.

More than an aesthetic style, International Style Modernist architecture symbolically expressed the "organization man" ideology of post-WWII corporate capitalism. As David Harvey explains in *The Condition of Postmodernity*, spatial practices "always express some kind of class or other social content", and the spatial practices of Modernist architecture and urbanism reflected the emerging ideology of post-WWII corporate America (239). Consequently, when jazz writers attacked post-WWII American cities with their "windy saxophone revolutions," "thousand saxophones infiltrat[ing] the city," and "eli eli lamma lamma sabacthani saxophone cr[ies] that shivered the cities," they attacked these cities not as a formally abstract physical spaces but rather as socio-spatial expressions of corporate ideologies (Kaufman, *Cranial Guitar*, 102; Kaufman, "Battle Report," 8; Ginsberg 131). The second section of "Howl," in particular, criticizes how the capitalist political economy imposed its political values onto urban spaces by constantly intermingling negative references to corporate America's "unobtainable dollars," "skeleton treasuries," "running money," and "banks" among its harsh critique of post-WWII urban redevelopment:

> Moloch whose buildings are judgment! . . . Robot apartments! invisible suburbs!
> . . . invincible mad houses! granite cocks! . . . They broke their backs lifting Moloch
> to Heaven! Pavements, trees, radios, tons! lifting the city to Heaven which exists
> and is everywhere about us! (Ginsberg 131–2)

As Ginsberg's oscillation between corporate America's "unobtainable dollars" and post-WWII American cities' "granite cocks" and "invisible suburbs" demonstrates, the political economy of corporate capitalism significantly influenced post-WWII urban redevelopment. By representing the inextricable web that connected the socio-spatial restructuring of post-WWII New York City with the capitalist political economy that financed it, Ginsberg demonstrates how corporate architecture functions as a symbolic barometer of socio-economic trends because of the "virtually unmediated relationship" that exists between architectural practices and the economic interests that finance them (Jameson 5).

Consequently, post-WWII jazz writers used critical representations of architectural and urban spaces both to decipher and to critique the political ideology of the material culture that produced them. This helps explain both the source of post-WWII jazz writers' antagonism toward cities and their reason for turning to jazz as a counter-hegemonic alternative urban paradigm. They promoted jazz's ecstatic, fragmented, disjunctive, and polymorphic "liquid geometry" as an alternative to the "pure geometry" of International Style Modernist architecture and its "square" corporate ideologies. They used the complex melodies and harmonies of jazz as a metaphor for new non-linear, anti-functionalist, and self-consciously heterogeneous urban paradigms. Post-WWII jazz writers also recognized in jazz musicians' flamboyant pork-pie hats, berets, and goatees a cultural critique of corporate America's sober gray flannel suits and unornamented geometrical architecture. They considered modern jazz's emphasis on creative improvisation as a political challenge to post-WWII America's deference to social conventions and hierarchical institutional directives. In short, jazz music, jazz clubs, and jazz culture provided jazz writers with both an aesthetic and a political alternative to the rigid socio-spatial practices and corporate ideologies that International Style Modernist architecture inscribed onto the urban space of post-WWII New York City. An excellent example of the kind of alternative "liquid geometries" promoted by the cultural avant-garde can be seen in Norman Mailer's Lego-block model of his proposed 15,000–unit apartment building. Fragmenting and complicating the "pure geometry" of International Style Modernism in the same way that bebop jazz complicated standard melodies and traditional chord structures, Mailer's proposal illustrated the more complex, heterogeneous kinds of spatial practices advocated by the New York avant-garde.

It should come as no surprise, therefore, that many of the Beat writers who first developed this sense of jazz as an alternative urban paradigm—such as Holmes, Kaufman, Ginsberg, and Joans—directed their urban critique specifically against corporate skyscrapers' socio-spatial domination of post-WWII urban space. For example, Kaufman's "J'Accuse" accuses the city of being a "jealous bitch, / purposely growing skyscraping office buildings / on the vacant lots in which we offered each other / as one singular tribute, to our personal star" (*Cranial Guitar*, 156), while Ginsberg's "Howl" criticizes the city of "Moloch whose skyscrapers stand in the long streets like endless Jehovahs" and whose "sphinx[es] of cement and aluminum bashed open [the] skulls" and "ate up [the] brains and imagination" of his generation (131). Joans's skyscraper-poem, "Sky High," also condemns skyscrapers for their life-negating "cold," "grey," and "tombstone[-like]" presence. In another jazz "take" on corporate architecture, Joans criticizes the "modern impressionist jazz pianist Bill Evans" by comparing him to a "white urban skyscraper wide street concrete park soul pouring forth" (*A Black Manifesto*, 40). Common to all three writers' critique of skyscraper architecture, therefore, is a sense that skyscrapers impose not only their physical presence but also their dehumanizing techno-rational and corporate ideologies onto the urban spaces and urban subjects that they dominate. These writers all represent corporate architecture not as an ideologically neutral physical space but rather as a material inscription of particular psychological states and social values.

RADICALIZING JAZZ LITERATURE: FROM THE BEAT GENERATION TO THE BLACK ARTS MOVEMENT

> Although the speech-like attributes are perhaps less obvious in their work, this is also the significance of Coltrane's eerie shrieks and *basso profundo* explosions, the jagged bass clarinet squeals of Eric Dolphy, even the more stately and oblique lamentations of Ornette Coleman: all invoke, to one degree or another, those cadences and rhythms that are unique to the lives of black people in the urban environment.
> —Frank Kofsky, from *John Coltrane and the Jazz Revolution of the 1960s*

Much like the Beat Generation writers of the 1950s, the Black Arts writers of the 1960s and early 1970s also turned to jazz as a means of representing, analyzing, and imagining alternatives to the material restructuring of post-WWII American cities. Even though these Black Arts writers often shared the Beat Generation's sense of jazz as a quintessential expression of urban experience, their different relationships to both jazz and cities frequently caused them to take a more critical view of the relationship between jazz and urban space. For example, Baron James Ashanti's "Just Another Gig" describes a Charlie Parker "cutting session" as an "urban tragedy of feeling too much / becom[ing] inimitable art" (4), while Amiri Baraka's "AM/TRAK" describes the Coltrane-Davis collaborations of the late 1950s as "sum[ming] up life in the slick / street part of the / world" (3). As these poems demonstrate, Black Arts writers also recognized a strong connection between jazz and cities, but their understanding of this interrelationship was shaped by more politically engaged and racially specific urban agendas. For example, Larry Neal's "Don't Say Goodbye to the Pork-Pie Hat" describes jazz music as the "elegance of style / gleaned from the city's underbelly" (143), but he specifically situates this relationship between jazz and cities in the context of racial politics: "drift[ing] above the cities of Black America; / all over America black musicians are putting / on the pork-pie hat again, picking up their axes, / preparing to blow away the white dream" (145). Walter De Legall's "Psalm for Sonny Rollins" also describes jazz musicians picking up their "axes" to "blow down the Chicago citadels, / Of Convention," "blow down the Caucasian battlements / Of bigotry," and "[b]low down thunder and lightning / And White People!! Blow down moons / And stars and Christs!" (202). Even Thomas Pynchon's *Gravity's Rainbow* invokes this militaristic sense of jazz when it describes Charlie Parker's "KoKo" as "finding out how he can use the notes at the higher ends of these very chords to break up the melody into *have* mercy what is it a fucking machine gun or something he must be out of his *mind* 32nd notes demisemiquavers" (63). Considering the larger context in which this quotation appears, Pynchon's representation of Parker's music likely parodies Black Nationalist representations of jazz, but even as a parody it demonstrates that representations of jazz as a racially motivated, militant form of cultural critique constituted a distinctly recognizable literary genre by the early 1970s.

Taken collectively, these examples demonstrate how many Black Arts writers not only continued, but even extended, the Beat Generation's sense of jazz as a counter-hegemonic urban paradigm. Instead of simply criticizing International Style Modernism's geometrical aesthetics for symbolically expressing the "square" ideologies of corporate capitalism, Black Arts writers used jazz to attack the racial inequalities—the "white dream" and "Caucasian battlements / Of bigotry"—that pervaded post-WWII American urbanism's segregated spatial practices (Neal 145; De Legall 202). They explicitly racialized their sense of jazz as a counter-hegemonic urban paradigm both by associating jazz with "black musicians" and the "cities of Black America" on the one hand, and by directing their urban critique against the "sanctity of white / America" on the other (Neal 144–5). In particular, Neal's "Don't Say Goodbye to the Pork-Pie Hat" describes how black jazz musicians "blow away the white dream" with "crisp and moaning voices leaping in the horns of destruction, / blowing doom and death to all who have no use for the Spirit" (145). Askia Muhammad Touré's "Extension" also describes a "New Thing bursting out of Black saxaphones": the "Wild Song of the Black Heart: / E X T E N S I O N over the crumbling ghettoes, riding / the deep ominous night—the Crescent Moon, the Evening Star; / the crumbling ghettoes exploding exploding: BAROOM, BAROOM!" (305–06). Similarly, Sonia Sanchez's "a/coltrane/poem" describes John Coltrane's saxophone as a "screeeeeeeeeeeeeeeeeeCHHHHHHHHHHHH" aimed against the "WITE/LIBERALS" to "MAKE THEM / SCREEEEEEEAM" and "TOR-TURE / THEM FIRST AS THEY HAVE / TORTURED US WITH / PROMISES" (*We A BaddDDD People*, 70–71). With these racially-charged images, Black Arts writers depicted jazz not as an abstract opposi-tional aesthetic style but rather as a racially specific black counter-hege-monic political vision. As De Legall explains, jazz is a "vibrant, all-embrac-ing, all-pervading / Sound which bleeds from the vinylite veins / Of my record" and "steals into the conduits of my heart / Forces entry into the sanctuary / Of my soul, trespasses into the temple / Of my gonads" (202). Similarly, Carolyn Rodgers describes "pharaoh and trane playing in [her] guts" (35), while Touré associates "Black saxaphones" with "the Root, the Primeval things before the West . . . the call of your ancestors; FEEL / their cries within your bones, your blood, / within your hearts" ("Extension," 304–5). By using such bodily and historically grounded images to represent jazz, Black Arts writers connected jazz to specific personal and historical experiences from which its oppositional practices cannot be easily dissoci-ated. Drawing on this more Afrocentric understanding of the inextricable relationship between modern jazz, Afro-American history, and Black Nationalist politics, Black Arts writers used jazz to advocate more racially conscious urban political agendas.

On one level, this racialization of jazz simply reflected both Black Arts writers' greater sensitivity to the racial dynamics of jazz music and their interest in post-bop jazz's heightened exploration of Afrocentric musical forms and Black Nationalist politics, as exemplified by works such as Charles Mingus's "Freedom," Archie Shepp's *Yasmina/Poem for Malcolm*, and John Coltrane's "Alabama" or "Kulu Se Mama." At another level, however, Black Arts writers' Afrocentric sense of jazz also marked a signif-icant reconceptualization of how and why they used jazz to analyze post-WWII urban space. Instead of using jazz to critique the corporate ideology of International Style Modernist architecture like Beat writers did, Black Arts writers used jazz to politically challenge how the fundamental racial and class antagonisms of the capitalist political economy segregate post-WWII American cities. As Paul Virilio argues in "The Overexposed City," when cities are exposed to the "effects of a multinational economy modeled along the lines of industrial enterprises," the "frontiers of the State pass to the interior of the cities" (381). In other words, the evolving logic of post-WWII corporate capitalism restructured the socio-spatial topography of American cities to reflect the kinds of economic and political forces that have shaped the international conflicts between industrial and preindustrial nations or between colonial/neo-colonial powers and their colonies/post-colonies. While the radical homogeneous aesthetics of International Style Modernist architecture reflected one dimension of post-WWII corporate capitalism's hegemonic power, other bifurcating processes such as gentrification, suburbanization, and ghettoization expressed different kinds of race and class antagonisms that pervaded the capitalist political economy.

Using jazz to explore how post-WWII American cities functioned as a microcosm of the new global economy's inequities, contradictions, and violence, Black Arts writers focused their urban critique less on corporate America's domination of post-WWII urban space than on African American urban issues such as the unequal development, racial segregation, and violent policing of minority urban communities. For example, David Henderson's "Walk with De Mayor of Harlem" describes how refocusing one's attention on minority neighborhoods such as Harlem, instead of Manhattan's central business district, produces a "vertigo / under skyscrapers / where Harlem lies / find no industrial green / giants / only / bojangling children in the streets" (*De Mayor of Harlem*, 14). Touré's "JuJu" also describes how Harlem's "trash-blown streets" are "crushed against the Towers of the West," while its citizens' "blues-ridden hearts" struggle to "live dynamic in the Soul against the deadly / concrete and steel blaring trumpets" of the urban center (172–3). From these alternative African American perspectives, post-WWII New York City was less a city of homogeneous geometrical architecture than it was a bifurcated city sharply divided along racial and economic lines established by corporate capitalism's unequal distribution of material resources. For many Black Arts writers, post-WWII American cities were not bastions of radical conformity and homogeneity, but rather they were violent battlegrounds where disparate urban communities confronted each other across intractable barriers and insurmountable divides. Concurring with Michael Harrington's *The Other America* and the 1968 Report of the National Advisory Commission on Civil Disorders, Black Arts jazz writers explored how post-WWII American cities functioned as the front lines in a new urban civil war that was erupting between two racially and economically segregated urban worlds that were "black and white, separate, hostile, and unequal" (Kerner Commission 8).

In particular, these writers used their politicized and racialized sense of jazz to critique the de facto segregation of American cities, the "[a]ggregate contraction of the white population, and particularly of middle-income families, [which] was accompanied by a shift in its center of gravity to the more recently developed areas of Queens and Staten Island—New York City's internal suburbs" (Fainstein, Fainstein, and Schwartz 52–53). For example, Gil Scott-Heron's "Harlem: The Guided Tour" criticizes the white flight of "400,000 New Yorkers who loved / reality so much that they never want to see it again" and retreated instead to privileged suburban enclaves (*Small Talk at 125th and Lenox*, 25). Gwendolyn Brooks's "In the Mecca" also directs its readers to "[s]it where the light corrupts your face. / Mies Van der Rohe retires from grace. / And the fair fables fall" (5). Turning away from Miesian International Style architecture, Brooks focuses attention instead on the Mecca, a dilapidated inner-city Chicago apartment building where the Law unresponsively "trots about" and "pounds a dozen doors" after crimes are committed, and the residents "hate sewn suburbs, / hate everything combed and strong; hate people who / have balls, dolls, mittens and dimity frocks and trains / and boxing gloves, picture books, bonnets for Easter. / Lace handkerchief owners are enemies of Smithkind" (19, 10). Connecting their exploration of post-bop jazz to the racial and economic divisions that fragmented post-WWII American cities, these writers repeatedly represented jazz either as the anguished cries emerging from the "charred / cornices topping crosstown gutted buildings" in impoverished minority ghettos, or as the revolutionary songs that would "lift us high upon a hill above the ghetto death-traps / past Suffering and Want past Heartbreak and Heartache" with a "Coltrane spirit-song / to the birthing / Soul of a New World / a'Coming. / From the Pyramids to the Projects . . . we grow upwards & outwards" (Hull 88; Touré, "JuJu," 174; Touré, *From the Pyramids to the Projects*, 30). Whether as an "urban tragedy" of the "crumbling ghettoes exploding" or as revolutionary new sounds that would "drift above the cities of Black America . . . preparing to blow away the white dream," Black Arts writers explored how the aesthetics and politics of post-bop jazz were inextricably connected to an alternative Afrocentric understanding of urban space (Ashanti 4; Touré "Extension," 306; Neal 145). By depicting various kinds of apocalyptic black jazz urban spaces on the verge of either exploding into revolution or imploding into ruins, Black Arts writers used jazz not only to assert a sense of black national identity and to explore Afrocentric aesthetic forms, but also to develop an Afrocentric critique of post-WWII urbanism.

These representations of hard bop and avant-garde jazz as a materially grounded and politically engaged counter-hegemonic African American urban discourse strikingly resemble Frank Kofsky's interpretation of the 1960s black jazz avant-garde. As Kofksy explains:

if one listens with care and an open mind, what one will hear in the music of John
Coltrane, Eric Dolphy, Ornette Coleman, Sam Rivers, Pharoah Sanders, Albert Ayler
and especially Archie Shepp is not speech "in general," but the voice of the Negro
ghetto. . . . I maintain that Archie Shepp's growling raspy tenor saxophone locu-
tions, for example, distill the quintessence of Negro vocal patterns as they can be
heard on the streets of Chicago, Detroit, Philadelphia, Harlem, or wherever you
choose. Although the speech-like attributes are perhaps less obvious in their work,
this is also the significance of Coltrane's eerie shrieks and *basso profundo* explo-
sions, the jagged bass clarinet squeals of Eric Dolphy, even the more stately and
oblique lamentations of Ornette Coleman: all invoke to one degree or another,
those cadences and rhythms that are unique to the lives of black people in the
urban environment. (229–30)

When it was originally published in 1970, most jazz critics harshly criticized Kofsky's analysis for being too racially politicized, but many Black
Arts writers shared Kofsky's sense of post-bop jazz as a quintessential
expression of black urban experiences. For these writers, hard bop and
avant-garde jazz musicians did not invent new musical styles simply to
experiment with modernist and Afro-centric aesthetic forms, but instead
they also developed these innovative interart aesthetic practices both to
address particular urban issues and to advance specific urban political
agendas. They turned to jazz as an African American urban cultural discourse that could help them describe, analyze, and imagine alternatives to
the socio-spatial topography of their material urban environment.

Both the Beat writers of the 1950s and the Black Arts writers of the
1960s demonstrated the political significance of interart aesthetic practices
by using literary representations of jazz to explore urban issues, but their
different understandings of jazz and urban space caused them to develop
fundamentally different kinds of interart aesthetic practices. To understand
fully how post-WWII jazz literature invoked jazz to represent, analyze, and
re-imagine the material restructuring of post-WWII New York City, one
must look beneath the common consensus that jazz simply represented a
chaotic, complex, heterogeneous, counter-hegemonic urban paradigm.
Even though a wide range of post-WWII writers concurred that jazz
expressed some kind of alternative urban sensibility, these writers did not
always agree about the precise nature of this relationship between jazz and
urban space. Different writers either privileged different jazz styles or
offered conflicting interpretations of the same style, and they frequently
used jazz to advocate diverse urban agendas—some complementary, others
contradictory, and many split along racial lines. The primarily white Beat
writers of the 1950s turned largely to the ecstatic, spontaneous energy of
bebop jazz—and especially Charlie Parker's music—to critique post-WWII
corporate America's bureaucratic "organization man" conformity, "gray
flannel suit" sobriety, and radically homogeneous International Style
Modernist and suburban architecture. When they represented jazz as a

counter-hegemonic force that attacked post-WWII American urbanism, they did so to criticize how International Style Modernism inscribed corporate America's dominant "square" cultural consensus onto architectural and urban spaces (Ginsberg 131; Kaufman, "Battle Report," 110). The predominately black jazz writers of the 1960s, however, generally turned to the more politically motivated and explicitly Afro-centric styles of hard bop and avant-garde jazz—ranging from late Coltrane and Charlie Mingus to Sun Ra, Pharoah Sanders, and Archie Shepp—to advance more racially specific urban political agendas that focused primarily on issues such as segregation, underdevelopment, and police brutality.

Taken collectively, post-WWII jazz writers' diverse engagements with urban space neither promoted a specific kind of alternative jazz city nor advocated a particular political urban agenda. Instead, they produced what Michel Foucault's "Of Other Spaces" describes as a heterotopia: a "kind of effectively enacted utopia in which the real sites, all the other real sites that can be found within the culture, are simultaneously represented, contested, and inverted" (24). In this sense, post-WWII writers' explorations of alternative jazz spaces—beneath, above, within, beyond, against, and on the margins of the post-WWII American city—functioned as a critical urban discourse that represented, analyzed, and imagined alternatives to the historical evolution of American cities. Even if these jazz spaces never existed as actual material spaces on the streets of post-WWII New York City, or perhaps only flourished in small "Jazz corner[s] of life" on the city's margins, they still performed a significant cultural work by simultaneously representing, contesting, and inverting "all the other real sites that [could] be found" in post-WWII New York City, including its International Style Modernist corporate architecture, its sprawling affluent suburbs, its racially and economically segregated ghettoes, and the larger megalopolitan system that connected these disparate spaces into a complex—simultaneously homogeneous and heterogeneous—global city (Kaufman, *Cranial Guitar*, 102; Foucault, "Of Other Spaces," 24).

Chapter Four

"I am for an art that does something other than sit on its ass in a museum"

Envisioning Alternative Utopic Urban Spaces

> What was needed was a vernacular corresponding to the creatively messy New York environment to ventilate the concentrated Surrealist imagery of poems like "Hatred," "Easter," and "Second Avenue." . . . In the poems he was to write during the remainder of his life—from about 1954 to 1966, the year of his death—this vernacular took over . . . for the reader who turns to poetry as a last resort in trying to juggle the contradictory components of modern life into something like a livable space. That space, in Frank O'Hara's case, was not only the space of New York School painting but of New York itself, that kaleidoscopic lumber-room where laws of time and space are altered—where one can live a few yards from a friend whom one never sees and whom one would travel miles to visit in the country.
> —John Ashbery, from the Introduction to Frank O'Hara's *Collected Poems*

SINCE THE PUBLICATION OF JOHN BERNARD MYERS'S *THE POETS OF THE NEW YORK School* (1969), the critical reception of the New York poets—Frank O'Hara, John Ashbery, Barbara Guest, Kenneth Koch, and James Schuyler—has been framed largely in terms of two competing interpretations. On the one hand, critics such as Myers, Fred Moramarco, Terrence Diggory, and Marjorie Perloff have argued that the New York poets constitute a collective "coterie" based primarily on their common engagement with "the aesthetics, the people, the politics, the social life and the concerns of the New York art world" (7). Emphasizing how these poets "turn[ed] to the plastic arts for their cultural nourishment instead of the accessible currents of contemporary literature," Myers defines their aesthetic style by explicit analogy to the New York School of abstract expressionist painting, arguing that "O'Hara did the same for 'unofficial' American poetry" as Pollock did for American painting because the "courage, the capacity for risk which is the hallmark of Pollock's style, can equally be said of O'Hara's as a poet" (8, 17–18). Since the publication of Myers's work, several critics have expanded the scope and adjusted the focus of his original

argument, but they have largely followed his precedent of defining, interpreting, and analyzing the New York School of poetry in terms of various
interart analogies. For example, Marjorie Perloff's *Frank O'Hara: Poet
Among Painters* (1977) expands O'Hara's interart influences to include
"painting, sculpture, film, [and] music" (29), and it elaborates Myers's
analogy to the visual arts in more detail, comparing O'Hara's poetry to:

> such major concepts of Abstract Expressionism as "push and pull," "all-over paint-
> ing" (composition as continuum with no beginning or end), and Harold
> Rosenberg's famous observation that in Action Painting the canvas becomes an
> arena upon which to act rather than a space in which to reproduce. (85)

In her new introduction to the 1997 edition of *Frank O'Hara: Poet Among
Painters*, Perloff further adjusts her interart analogy by comparing
O'Hara's style to the Second Generation of New York School painters
instead of the original New York School of abstract expressionism:

> what has become apparent with the passage of time is that O'Hara's aesthetic is
> closer to the conceptualism of the John Cage—Merce Cunningham—Jasper Johns—
> Robert Rauschenberg circle of the fifties and sixties (a circle of gay, if notably clos-
> eted and discreet, artists) than to the openly emotive and expressive gestures of
> Action Painting or Black Mountain or Beat aesthetic. (xxiii)

While this new argument—which has also been advanced in various forms
by critics such as James Breslin, Charles Altieri, Geoffrey Ward, and David
Lehman—provides a more accurate and more subtle interpretation of the
New York poets, it retains the essence of Myers's original thesis: the New
York poets are still interpreted by means of some interart analogy to a par-
ticular movement in post-WWII New York art.

Another critical camp, however, interprets the New York poets in
terms of their collective engagement with the urban space of post-WWII
New York City. For example, Charles Altieri's *Enlarging the Temple* (1979)
argues that the "city is a perfect metaphor" for O'Hara's aesthetic style
because the everyday details of city life, like O'Hara's poetry, are "committed to perpetual change;" have no "meaning, hierarchy, nor purpose not
created absolutely by man;" and offer a "series of phenomena to notice,
perhaps to play with in one's own psyche, but very rarely do these phenomena inspire or welcome any attempt to participate in their lives"
(111–2). Noting that O'Hara was "fascinated by the city and saw in it not
only the potential for subject matter but also the opportunity for organiza-
tional strategies and perspectives new to poetry" (321), Neal Bowers's
"The City Limits" claims that O'Hara's *Collected Poems* literally:

is a city, as diverse and incoherent as any city is likely to be, and yet whole. In fact, it is useful to approach each O'Hara poem as a city—not as a microcosm but as that part of a city immediately available through the consciousness of Frank O'Hara, the part that contains the whole. (323)

While both critical camps tend to find similar characteristics in O'Hara's poetry—extreme linguistic fragmentation, ludic surrealistic imagery, and a passionate interest in the quiddity of the quotidian—they offer competing accounts of how to explain these characteristics. One group sees them as a textual translation of abstract expressionist or post-abstract-expressionist art, while the other group sees them as a linguistic approximation of the dynamic, chaotic rhythms of urban life.

Both groups, however, tend to produce one-dimensional interpretations that privilege some single, or at least primary, influence that can give order to the New York poets' radically heterogeneous poetic projects. In addition, both groups tend to reduce the New York poets to some more-or-less isomorphic, mechanical, passive reflection of whatever aesthetic or urban phenomenon they have privileged, instead of exploring how the New York poets enter into complex, creative, and productive exchanges with various kinds of practices. While no critical analysis can simultaneously bring into play every dimension of even one of the New York poets, let alone the collective range of the entire coterie, critics need to develop more pluralistic and comparative models that at least bring into play multiple dimensions of their work. Instead of looking for some final privileged influence or analogy that can explain the vast range of the New York poets' writing, critics need to analyze how these poets explore a wide range of influences, ranging from visual art and urban space to music and dance, and extending from the theoretical abstraction of abstract expressionist art to the pulp concreteness of cinematic images. What is most important in their work is perhaps not any single or dominant influence, but rather the complex intermixing of multiple influences in different and continually changing combinations. Moreover, instead of describing these influences as isomorphic processes, whereby the New York poets passively translate some particular non-literary influence into a more-or-less identical textual equivalent, these writers' interart aesthetic experiments explore a range of creative exchanges that redraw traditional disciplinary boundaries. As W. J. T. Mitchell has argued, *"comparison itself is not a necessary procedure"* in interdisciplinary analysis, but rather the "necessary subject matter" should be the:

whole ensemble of *relations* between media, and relations can be many things besides similarity, resemblance, and analogy. Difference is just as important as similarity, antagonism as crucial as collaboration, dissonance and division of labor as interesting as harmony and blending of function. (89–90)

Many analyses of the New York poets are methodologically flawed, not only because they emphasize a single privileged interdisciplinary comparison, but also because they are based on a reductive understanding of interdisciplinary influence.

This chapter advances a more pluralistic interpretation of the New York poets as a multi-dimensional coterie that not only engages a wide range of interdisciplinary influences but also does so through complex and creative exchanges that transcend passive and mechanical imitation. Howard Kanovitz's painting, *The New Yorkers* (1967), presents an excellent visual illustration of what this kind of multi-dimensional interpretation of the New York poets might be like.

Instead of depicting O'Hara as a derivative imitator of some group of visual artists, as many critical interpretations either assert or imply, this painting represents O'Hara at the center of a group of New York artists and intellectuals who seemingly revolve around his powerful presence. At the same time that this painting emphasizes O'Hara's central, as opposed to peripheral, position within the post-WWII New York avant-garde, it also suggests O'Hara's pervasive interdisciplinarity by surrounding him with an interdisciplinary circle that includes the composer Morton Feldman, the art critics Sam Hunter and B. H. Friedman, and the painters Larry Rivers, Alex Katz, and Howard Kanovitz. Like the other New York poets, O'Hara not only moved freely within a wide-ranging interdisciplinary circle, but he was also a productive cultural agent who creatively extended, challenged, and reconfigured these numerous interart influences.

Instead of either debating whether the city or the visual arts provides the best analogy for O'Hara's poetry or defining some single visual aesthetic as the definitive analogy that best explains O'Hara's work, I will explore instead how the New York poets develop a wide range of aesthetic practices by experimenting with different combinations of experimental aesthetic strategies modeled after both the complex visual aesthetics of modern art and the heterogeneous socio-spatial topography of post-WWII New York City. Even though the two primary competing interpretations of the New York poets share many family resemblances that recur throughout the critical literature, occasionally even crossing paths within the same critical essay, few critics have systematically analyzed the relationship between these two fundamentally interrelated aspects of the New York poets' work. They have neither explained how the New York poets' immersion in the New York art world shapes their sense of New York City as an urban space, nor conversely how the New York poets' sense of urban space colors their interpretations of modern art. However, one aspect that defines these poets—both as a collective coeterie with a shared aesthetic agenda and as a unique coterie that is distinct from its artistic counterparts and urban context—is precisely the way that these poets bring both the city and its artistic culture together into a provocative and creative dialogue. The New York poets do not simply translate visual aesthetics into textual forms any more than they merely express the complex rhythms of urban life. Rather, they explore, extend, synthesize, and modify a wide range of artistic and urban issues to create complex explorations of the "ar(t)chitextural" interrelationship between visual, spatial, and textual practices. Like

Howard Kanovitz. *The New Yorkers,* 1967. Collection of Mr. and Mrs. Earl McGrath, New York City. (Reprinted with permission of Mr. and Mrs. Earl McGrath).

post-WWII jazz writers' repeated explorations of the relationship between jazz and urban space, the New York poets simultaneously engage both the arts and the city to explore various interrelationships between visual and urban practices. It is these interrelationships—more than the visual aesthetics of modern art or the urban space of post-WWII New York City in isolation—that shape many of the New York poets' most interesting works.

An excellent example of this can be seen in the work of Barbara Guest and Frank O'Hara. Like the other New York School poets, these two writers not only explore a wide range of interart influences, but they also repeatedly connect their interart experiments with critical analyses of architectural and urban spaces. At the same time that these writers share a common project of simultaneously exploring both visual and spatial issues in their writing, they develop distinct variations on these themes. In particular, Guest's writing frequently uses aesthetic strategies modeled after modernist visual art to represent precarious, eccentric poetic spaces, but it often privileges modern art over spatially derived aesthetic practices grounded in the daily rhythms of urban life. Her writing creates a bridge between artistic and spatial practices, but the traffic on that bridge primarily travels in one direction. She represents modernist and abstract expressionist spaces that are strongly influenced by the visual arts, but she rarely develops an alternative, spatially grounded or urban-inflected sense of modernist art. Her writing explores both visual and spatial practices, but there tends to be a relatively homogeneous, isomorphic correspondence between these two dimensions of her work. Both her interart references to the visual arts and her spatial imagery generally share a rather orthodox modernist sense of spatial and textual fragmentation, discontinuity, and simultaneity.

Like Guest, O'Hara also repeatedly connects his interest in complex, heterogeneous urban spaces to his exploration of textual-visual interart aesthetics, but he simultaneously intensifies and fuses these two dimensions of his work in a way that makes their interaction more dynamic than it is in Guest's writing. Not only does he develop two distinct, though interrelated, artistic and urban sensibilities, but the sometimes subtle and at other times antagonistic differences between these two dimensions of his work enable him to explore a more complex range of spatial and textual possibilities. Some of his poems tend more toward the complex, fragmented visual aesthetics of modernist art, while other poems conform more closely to the dynamic rhythms of quotidian urban life. Sometimes his poetry synthesizes new hybrid combinations of visual and spatial forms, while at other times it explores the antagonisms, gaps, tensions, and discontinuities that emerge between them. Constantly exploring new interrelationships between visual and spatial practices, O'Hara's poetry develops one of the most comprehensive examples of how post-WWII New York writers simultaneously explored a wide range of interart aesthetic practices and critically analyzed the complex socio-spatial topography of the city's heterogeneous urban spaces.

"LITERATURE AS DESTRUCTION OF SPACE": THE PRECARIOUS ARCHITECTURE OF BARBARA GUEST'S SPATIAL IMAGINATION

> Literature as destruction of space.
> —Barbara Guest, from *Seeking Air*

Critics have long noted that spatial images and themes play a central role in Guest's writing. For example, Anthony Manousos argues that *The Location of Things* (1960) "focuses primarily on spatial metaphors. In a sense, it deals with distances—physical, aesthetic, personal—that each individual must somehow confront" (296). Barbara Hillman also describes how Guest's poetry explores the "tension between different types of reality, different types of location" in order to produce poems that are "geographically ambiguous," and she identifies "space, light, and air" as three of Guest's major themes (210–11). Even a cursory glance at the titles of Guest's poems immediately reveals her interest in spatial imagery. Poems such as "The Location of Things," "The Screen of Distance," and "Direction" explicitly announce themselves as explorations of spatiality, while "The Blue Stairs," "Piazzas," "The Farewell Stairway," and "Turkey Villas" describe particular kinds of architectural spaces. Even a poem like "The Hero Leaves His Ship," which seems to have nothing to do with space, invokes architectural images such as the apartments' "precarious architecture" and the "roof [that] will hold me" in order to develop its themes (*Poems*, 20–21). In the process of reading Guest's work, readers encounter numerous doors, windows, stairs, roofs, walls, rooms, houses, buildings, streets, art studios, museum galleries, and other kinds of spaces, and these poetic spaces frequently rank among Guest's most striking and distinctive images.

Despite the prevalence of these spatial images, critics have not sufficiently analyzed how these poetic spaces function in Guest's writing. Much more remains to be said about both how and why spatial images ubiquitously pervade her writing. What kind of space does she attempt to construct with these images, and why is it so fragmented, chaotic, and abstract? Is there a "structure" to this space, or does it intimate an absence or impossibility of structure, or does it imagine some kind of alternative, negative, or irreducibly heterogeneous spatial possibility? Moreover, do these spatial images have aesthetic consequences? Are they essential or merely accidental to her larger aesthetic project? Does she explore "architextural" relationships between the structure of these spatial images and the structure of her experimental textual aesthetics? Finally, what kind of

cultural or rhetorical work do these spatial images perform? Are they purely decorative and aesthetic, or do they belong to some larger social or political project? In short, why do these spatial images matter? What aesthetic,
cultural, or political issues do they engage? To some extent, this critical
lacuna simply continues a general pattern of critical neglect of Guest's
work, but it also prevents critics from understanding the full significance of
her larger aesthetic project—both because her work includes a wide range
of spatial images and because Guest herself repeatedly suggests that particular spaces, spatial images, and the concept of spatiality fundamentally
inform her personal aesthetic vision. Given that Guest's writing frequently
emphasizes both spatial imagery and aesthetic issues, it is less surprising
that spatial images play a crucial role in defining her aesthetic sensibility
than that critics have not analyzed either how these poetic spaces shape her
aesthetic practices or what kind of cultural work is performed by them.

In her own critical and literary works, Guest both explicitly and
implicitly describes how her aesthetic experimentation is intimately connected to her creative examination of spatial forms. Her essay, "A Reason
for Poetics," describes her writing as exploring a "pull in both directions
between the physical reality of place and the metaphysics of space. This
pull will build up a tension within the poem giving a view of the poem from
both the interior and the exterior" (153). Here Guest sees her own writing
as oscillating between two spatial poles: sometimes it represents the reality
of particular physical places, while at other times it develops a more philosophical interrogation of spatiality as a theoretical concept. In her poem,
"The Screen of Distance," Guest further associates poetic and spatial forms
by describing how a "difficult poem intrudes like hardware / decorating a
quiet building, a tic taking / over the façade, a shrug exaggerated by a / col-
umn" (*Collected Poems*, 136). This poem also interweaves various images
of spatial and poetic construction by depicting the "sonorous / movement
of a poem" as the "ego of words stretched to / the room's borders" and by
describing how narratives occupy a "room where the screen waits suspended like / the frame of a girder the worker will place upon / an axis and
thus make a frame which he fills with / a plot or a quarter inch of poetry
to encourage / nature into his building" (132). While readers often tacitly
assume that both poems and narratives are constructed in some sense,
Guest's images not only make this association between poetic and architectural construction explicit, but they also characterize the relationship
between spaces and texts according to a complex modernist spatial-textu-
al logic. It is one thing to describe a poem as well-wrought or a narrative
as a structure that moves deliberately from beginning to middle to end, but
Guest's imagery suggests that literature is constructed according to much
more unpredictable models, which vary from being "suspended" at one
moment to being a "quarter inch" thick at another.

Many of Guest's poems use spatial images to explore aesthetic issues. For example, "The Blue Stairs" creates a complex analogy between "master builder[s]" and "artists" confronted with similar challenges, and it develops this analogy by repeatedly oscillating between "spatially selective" descriptions of a "ladder," an "elevator," "stairs," "secret platforms," and the "republic of space," on the one hand, and a theoretical discussion of how and why "work[s] of art" are "framed," "beautiful," and "excellen[t]," on the other hand (*The Blue Stairs*, 3–6). As James Atlas explains, Guest's blue staircase functions as an "excuse for aesthetics, to be read 'with a heavy and pure logic.' [. . .] It is only when the poet departs from the limitations of describing perception and arrives at perception itself that she achieves her most accomplished work" (quoted in Manousos 298). The title of "Piazzas" also suggests that it is a poem about a particular kind of architectural space, but Manousos notes that this poem simultaneously develops a "dazzling meditation on the ambiguous transformations of art that seems to anticipate, in miniature, Ashbery's 'Self-Portrait in a Convex Mirror'" (298). In other words, Guest's poems depict various kinds of spatial images and architectural spaces, but they do so in part to explore aesthetic issues. In particular, her novel, *Seeking Air*, explicitly and provocatively suggests how spatiality plays a central role in her conception of writing. Embedded within a series of stream-of-consciousness associations, Guest's narrator, Morgan Flew, describes literature as the "destruction of space" (160). In this enigmatic aphorism, Guest succinctly encapsulates the broader aesthetic significance of her critical exploration of spatial forms: her spatial images aggressively confront and challenge conventional notions of space, and this critical deconstruction of space plays a crucial role in her notion of what it means to write. Given these recurring associations between literature, aesthetics, art, and space, one cannot fully understand Guest's aesthetic project without explaining both how she represents various kinds of poetic spaces and how she relates these unorthodox poetic spaces to larger aesthetic issues regarding the nature and function of the aesthetic imagination.

Yet simply recognizing *that* Guest's spatial images play a crucial role in her work still does not explain exactly *how* or *why*. Even after noticing that spatial images recur throughout her work, one must still make sense of these poetic spaces, which are often highly abstract, ambiguous, and enigmatic. Attempting to analyze Guest's spatial images can initially make her writing seem more rather than less confusing precisely because these spatial images constitute some of the most complex aspects of her work. For example, "History," a poem written for Frank O'Hara, invokes spaces as diverse as "that pale refrigerator," the "wild woodbine landscapes," "those frozen tubs," and the "buttresses" of the "Church of Our Lady" to discuss not only history but also Guest's personal and artistic relationship with

O'Hara (*Poems*, 41). Even taken individually, these spatial images are peculiar, but it is even more difficult to comprehend the spatial logic that connects them—either to each other or to Guest's themes of history, friendship, and poetry. Similarly, the various stairs, ladders, elevators, platforms, and other spaces described in "The Blue Stairs" are obviously central images in this poem, but the poem never really clarifies either what these ambiguous and confusing poetic spaces really are or how they are supposed to function within the poem. Are these spaces real, metaphorical, imaginative, aesthetic, or textual? And how stable are these spaces if someone is "kicking the ladder away," the elevator is of the "most delicate / fixity," and even after "having reached the summit" it may be that the "stairs are withdrawn" (*The Blue Stairs*, 4–6)? Do these spatial structures allegorize some ultimate, grounded vision of truth, or do they simply reflect glimpses of an ephemeral, transitory, and esoteric consciousness or the endlessly deferring play of linguistic meaning? What sense can be made of Guest's spaces, especially when so many of them are eccentric, ambiguous, confusing, curiously unlocatable, or heterogeneously juxtaposed with other unusual spaces within the same poem? Ultimately, Guest's spatial images collectively invoke an unconventional and unsettling sense of space, or even a confusing web of intermingled heterogeneous spaces, which is very different from the secure and intimate spaces described by Gaston Bachelard in *The Poetics of Space*. Guest's spaces provide neither an "intimate, concrete essence that would be a justification of the uncommon value of all our images of protected intimacy," nor a "body of images that give mankind proofs or illusions of stability" (3, 17). In fact, most of Guest's spaces are precisely the opposite: they are spaces deliberately constructed both to unsettle conventional expectations about the nature of spatiality itself and to suggest instead intimations of a more complex world in which both "proofs" and "illusions" of "stability" are subverted by a profound awareness of the chaotic contingencies of modern life.

In this respect, Guest's spatial images are not altogether different from the rest of her poetic images. Yet, even though many of her other images are equally ambiguous, readers often find her ambiguous spatial images especially unsettling partly because they are traditionally accustomed to think of spaces as a privileged ground of stable meaning. Most critics now recognize that works of art, poetic texts, and linguistic signs can yield multiple interpretations. As Jacques Derrida explains, texts can be reinterpreted according to a "second interpretation of interpretation" characterized by a:

> Nietzschean *affirmation*, that is the joyous affirmation of the play of the world and of the innocence of becoming, the affirmation of a world of signs without fault, without truth, and without origin which is offered to an active interpretation. *This affirmation then determines the noncenter otherwise than as a loss of the center.*

> And it plays without security. For there is a *sure* play: that which is limited to the *substitution* of *given* and *existing, present,* pieces. In absolute chance, affirmation also surrenders itself to *genetic* indetermination, to the *seminal* adventure of the trace. (292)

Within such a Nietzschean hermeneutics of suspicion, stable one-to-one correspondences between signs and referents give way to a less certain and more aleatory play of language. It is often more difficult, however, to extend this Nietzschean "affirmation of the play of the world" to what Guest refers to as the "physical reality of place" because our commonsense understanding of space almost invariably reduces it to a "strictly geometrical meaning" based solely on "'Euclidean,' 'isotropic,' or 'infinite'" concepts that are ultimately "mathematical" (Lefebvre 1). But it is precisely this grounded and stable sense of space that Guest resists by exploring the tension between the "physical reality of place" and what she calls the "metaphysics of space," or the conceptual models and spatial regimes that organize our understanding of space ("A Reason for Poetics," 154). Guest's unconventional spatial images are not simply mimetic representations of physical places but rather metaphysical investigations of both how we construct spatiality and how we might imagine alternative spatial practices. While many of Guest's uncertain, ambiguous, polysemantic, and stream-of-consciousness images require her readers to adopt more Nietzschean-Derridean hermeneutic models, Guest's spatial images impel her readers to extend this same hermeneutics of suspicion to the "metaphysics of space" in order to deconstruct essentialized notions of the "physical reality of place." The critical crux of interpreting Guest's spatial images, therefore, lies in finding a way to enter into each poem's unconventional spatial logic without needing to reconfigure that poem's unique poetic spaces according to the reader's Euclidean spatial preconceptions. Instead, Guest challenges her readers to question, expand, and imagine alternatives to Euclidean spatiality.

In many ways, Guest's unorthodox spatial imagination emerges out of her interest in modernist painting and its radical reconceptualization of Renaissance perspectivism in the visual arts. If there is any common conceptual grounding for Guest's unorthodox spatial images it is the complex spatial practices developed by European modernist artists, such as Pablo Picasso and Juan Miró, and then later extended by American Abstract Expressionists, such as Grace Hartigan and Robert Motherwell. As Kathleen Fraser explains, Guest often appropriates "visual solutions proposed by European and American artists who prefigured (and influenced) abstract expressionism" in order to "create a disrupted narrative text" through a "strikingly innovative fictional model based on discrete units and intervals, strengthened by peculiar juxtapositions that resemble certain Cubist paintings or experimental films in their overlapping planes and

abrupt shifts" (240–1). In particular, modernist painting significantly influences Guest's unconventional spatial imagination because modernist experiments in the visual arts helped radically reconceptualize traditional
assumptions about the nature of spatiality. As Sigfried Giedion explains,
from the "Renaissance to the first decade of the present century perspective
had been one of the most important constituent facts in painting," but "in
modern art, for the first time since the Renaissance, a new conception of
space leads to a self-conscious enlargement of our ways of perceiving space.
It was in cubism that this was most fully achieved" (435–6). More specifically, Giedion argues that the "method of presenting spatial relationships
which the cubists developed led up to the form-giving principles of the new
space conception" because cubism views "objects relatively; that is, from
several points of view, no one of which has exclusive authority" (Giedion
434, 436). Consequently, cubism's "presentation of objects from several
points of view introduces a principle which is intimately bound up with
modern life—simultaneity," and the "essence of space as it is conceived
today is its many-sidedness, the infinite potentiality for relations within it"
(Giedion 435–6). In the same sense that Giedion claims that "no one can
understand contemporary architecture, become aware of the feelings hid-
den behind it, unless he [or she] has grasped the spirit animating this [mod-
ernist] painting," a similar argument can be made about the poetic strategies of many modernist poets and especially of New York School poets
such as Guest who so extensively engage the visual aesthetics of modernist
art (Giedion 433).

In many of her poems, Guest explicitly associates her spatial images
with references to modernist painting in order to explore alternative spatial
practices developed by modernist visual artists. In *Seeking Air*, for example, Morgan Flew comes to recognize that beneath the "extraordinary disorder" that Miriam leaves behind, there is a "lucidity in [her] placing of
personal objects" that resembles "Matisse's painting of 'Studio'"(14). As
this reference to Matisse demonstrates, Guest not only associates spaces of
"extraordinary disorder" with modernist painting, but she also invokes
Matisse's visual aesthetics to legitimate the "lucidity" of Miriam's disorderly sense of space. If readers approach Guest's spatial images with the
same rectilinear spatial perspective that Morgan initially brings to Miriam's
"extraordinary disorder," however, they will fail to see the "lucidity" of
Guest's aesthetic project. The deeper significance of Guest's spatial images
lies precisely in their ability to break down the reader's Euclidean spatial
preconceptions, in the same way that Matisse and other modernist painters
challenged the privileging of Renaissance perspectivism in the visual arts.
Readers must willfully suspend their conventional spatial expectations in
order to perceive the "lucidity" of Guest's disorderly poetic spaces and
alternative spatial paradigms. Similarly, "In the Middle of the Easel" con-

tends that "only / a cubist angle seen after / produces this volume in which our hearts go / (tick tick)," and the poem goes on to describe how cubist painters actively construct alternative spatial paradigms. Instead of confining their aesthetic vision within the rectilinear geometry of Renaissance perspectivism, they "disarray / in the twilight those boulevards" represented in their art (*Poems*, 23). This visual *disarraying* of Parisian boulevards provides an excellent visual analogue to Guest's own description of literature as the "*destruction* of space" (*Seeking Air*, 160, emphasis added). What Guest's spatial images are trying to accomplish aesthetically is to translate modernist artists' visual disarraying of space into literary practices that produce a similar unsettling of spatial structures.

Moreover, Guest's repeated associations between the alternative spatiality of "cubist angle[s]" and "disarray[ed]" boulevards on the one hand, and the "volume," "rapture," and "laughter" they provoke on the other hand, confirms Daniel Belgrad's claim that avant-garde artists forsake the "topical nature of realist art in favor of the more 'abstract' project of transforming the viewer's awareness" (*Poems*, 23; Belgrad 21). Guest does turn toward modernist painting and its alternative spatial sensibility as an inspiration for her own aesthetic style, but she does so in order to transform not only the aesthetic but also the epistemological and socio-political sensibilities of her readers. Her writing performs a certain kind of material cultural work by translating modernist visual and spatial aesthetics into literary forms, and the broader implications of this transformation are clearly evident in the contrast between the eccentric spatial imagery that pervades her writing and the occasional glimpse that she provides of more conventional spatial structures.

While most of Guest's spatial images are complex, disorderly, and enigmatic, there are a few places in which she represents more rigid geometrical spaces. For example, "Seeing You Off" depicts New York City's "continental factories" and "edens / of soap and fats" as the "splendors [that] make rigid a democracy / define its skeleton" (*Poems*, 30). Similarly, "Walking Buddha" refers to the "bronze asperity / essentials of being classical / in a violent world before the decline," while "Belgravia" describes a house "mileposts cut into the marble, / A block, ten blocks, a mile / For the one who walks here always thinking, / Who finds a meaning at the end of a mile / And wishes to entomb his discoveries" (*Selected Poems*, 41; *Poems*, 49). In each case, Guest associates a sense of spatial inflexibility and geometric precision—or Le Corbusier's "pure geometry"—with various kinds of intellectual monotony, political stagnation, and geopolitical violence. While it is true that social and political practices are not spatial structures in any literal sense, readers should not find it surprising that Guest's spatial imagination might associate rigid geometrical spaces with many of post-WWII America's most destructive social and political ideologies, such as the hyperconformity promoted by its dominant "square" culture, the political polarization produced by its "right-wing" McCarthyist paranoia and Cold War geopolitics, the patriarchal and heteronormative conventions disseminated by its "straight" gender politics, the rigid bureaucratization of its hierarchical corporate "organization man" culture, the radical spatial homogeneity of its suburban "little boxes made of ticky-tacky," and the "pure geometry" of its International Style Modernist glass-and-steel-box corporate architecture.

In opposition to these rigid social structures and architectural and urban spaces, Guest's writing attempts to imagine more complex literary spaces or "chamber[s] of ambiguity / where two equals may meet before disappearing" (*Collected Poems*, 35). Even though Guest's writing infrequently raises these social and political issues, at least in any explicitly political manner, the "precarious architecture" of her spatial imagination extends far beyond mimetic representations of the "physical reality of place." It also encompasses both a complex exploration of the aesthetic and philosophical "metaphysics of space" and a critical awareness of how spatial practices reflect, encode, engage, and imagine alternatives to particular social and political antagonisms. Through its "cubist angles," "extraordinary disorders," "chamber[s] of ambiguity," and other "destruction[s] of space," the "precarious architecture" of Barbara Guest's spatial imagination promotes a wide ranging experimentation with modernist spatial and social practices.

"Everything / suddenly honks: it is 12:40 of / a Thursday": Frank O'Hara's New York Sublime

> It's my lunch hour, so I go
> for a walk among the hum-colored
> cabs. First, down the sidewalk
> where laborers feed their dirty
> glistening torsos sandwiches
> and Coca-Cola, with yellow helmets
> on. . . .
>   Everything
> suddenly honks: it is 12:40 of
> a Thursday.
>   —Frank O'Hara, from "A Step Away From Them"

O'Hara's poetry, on the other hand, develops a more complex and multidirectional interaction between modern art and urban space because it is as intensely immersed in urban spaces as it is in modernist art. Instead of simply producing chaotic spatial images largely modeled after the fragmented visual aesthetics of modernist art, O'Hara's poetry moves in two distinct, though interrelated, directions. Sometimes it shifts closer to the visual aesthetics of modernist art, while other times it is more strongly influenced by the complex socio-spatial topography of urban spaces. Like the other New York poets, O'Hara was intimately involved in the post-WWII New York art world, but his aesthetic sensibilities are also profoundly shaped by the dynamic rhythms of urban life. For example, his prose-poem, "Meditations in an Emergency," declares, "I have never clogged myself with the praises of a pastoral life" because one "need never leave the confines of New York to get all the greenery one wishes—I can't even enjoy a blade of grass unless I know there's a subway handy, or a record store or some other sign that people do not totally *regret* life" (*Collected Poems*, 197). Similarly, "To the Mountains in New York" describes how he is "dropping [his] pastoral pretensions" and letting his "flock run around" because his "master died in [his] heart. / On the molten streets of New York / the master put up signs of my death. / I love this hairy city. / It's wrinkled like a detective story / and noisy and getting fat and smudged / lids hood the sharp hard black eyes" (*Collected Poems*, 198). In "Walking," he extends this urban sensibility into a full-blown urban sublime, arguing that the "country is no good for us" because "there's nothing / to bump into / or fall glassily apart / there's not enough / poured concrete / and brassy / reflections" (*Collected Poems*, 476–77). As in Guest's writing, the complex, heterogeneous urban topography of O'Hara's "wrinkled" city with "molten streets" full of obstacles and potential accidents clearly opposes the neo-Corbusian "pure geometry" of post-WWII American urbanism. Yet there is a sense in which O'Hara grounds his writing more concretely in the quotidian quiddity of urban space than Guest does. Perhaps O'Hara's celebrations of "molten" and "hairy" urban spaces are colored by his modernist aesthetic sensibility, but there is also a sense in which these poems have a greater density of "poured concrete," "record stores," and other "glassy" urban spaces to "bump into." Unlike Guest's poetry, which seems more of a one-dimensional translation of modernist artistic practices into spatial forms, O'Hara's poetry simultaneously engages the complexity of both modernist art and urban space. While some O'Hara poems move closer toward one extreme or the other, other O'Hara poems explore either synthetic fusions of or antagonistic tensions between diverse visual and spatial practices.

For example, a surrealist and abstract expressionist poem like "Second Avenue" moves more toward the visual aesthetics of modernist art, even though it strives to develop some kind of "ar(t)chitextural" relationship between art and urban space. As O'Hara explains in his "Notes on Second Avenue," this poem explores his experience of a particular urban space: "actually everything in it either happened to me or I felt happening (saw, imagined) on Second Avenue" (*Collected Poems*, 497). O'Hara specifically interprets the following passage as a description of "a woman I saw leaning out a window on Second Avenue with her arms on a pillow" (497):

> You remained for me a green Buick of sighs, o Gladstone!
> and your wife Trina, how like a yellow pill on a sill
> in the many-windowed dusk where the air is compartmented!
> her red lips of Hollywood, soft as a Titian and as tender,
> her grey face which refrains from thrusting aside the mane
> of your languorous black smells the hand crushed by her chin,
> and that slumberland of dark cutaneous lines which reels
> under the burden of her many-darkly-hued corpulence of linen
> and satin bushes, is like a lone rose with the sky behind it.
> A yellow rose. Valentine's Day. (*Collected Poems*, 147)

As the fragmented textual structure of this passage demonstrates, O'Hara's language attempts to emulate the complex, heterogeneous topography of New York City. Like so many O'Hara poems, however, the language oscillates ambivalently between modernist and urban influences. Not only does O'Hara's "actual" urban experience take constant detours into artistic milieus—pausing to "talk with a sculptor (Larry Rivers, who also sculpts) about a piece in progress" or present a "description of a Grace Hartigan painting"—but it also shifts back and forth between what "actually" happened and what O'Hara "imagined" happening on Second Avenue (496–7). The poem careens wildly between the "pelt of the whole city mov[ing] forward as a flame" and the "inky clarity" of a surrealist space that has "lines, cuts, drips, aspirates, trembles with horror" or a de Kooning-esque representation of "where the torrent has subsided at the very center / of classicism" (142, 149–50). Even O'Hara's explanation of the woman leaning out the window in this poem changes rapidly from a description of a "de Kooning WOMAN which I'd seen recently at his studio," to a description of a "woman that I saw leaning out a window on Second Avenue," to a description of a real woman but "the way it's done is influenced by de K's woman" (497). It is as if O'Hara cannot decide whether his poem should describe a painting or a city, and it is precisely this constant oscillation between—as opposed to the mere imitation of either—artistic practices and urban spaces that emerges as the real signatorial gesture in O'Hara's work. Even in "Second Avenue"—one of O'Hara's most surrealist, fragmented, abstract expressionist poems—he still makes an effort to explore some material relationship between its modernist-art-inspired visual-textual aesthetic experimentation and the sociospatial topography of the city.

In different O'Hara poems, however, this "ar(t)chitextural" interrelationship between the visual aesthetics of modernist art, the spatial structure of the city, and O'Hara's own experimentation with new textual strategies takes on different forms. While a poem like "Second Avenue" veers sharply toward the visual aesthetics of surrealism with only a few fragmentary urban spaces to bump into, a poem like O'Hara's "The Day Lady Died" grounds its aesthetics more firmly in his individual urban experience of "12:20 in New York a Friday / three days after Bastille day, yes / it is 1959 and I go get a shoeshine / because I will get off the 4:19 in Easthampton / at 7:15 and then go straight to dinner" (*Collected Poems*, 325). It makes less frequent references to "what the poets / in Ghana are doing these days" or the "little Verlaine / for Patsy," and it keeps much of its modernist fragmentation in check (325). In both its spatial and its textual structures, the poem closely follows the poet's quotidian urban itinerary through the "muggy streets" of Midtown Manhattan as he stops to get a "hamburger and a malted" or pick up a bottle of Strega at the "PARK LANE / Liquor Store" before returning to "6th Avenue / and the tobacconist in the Ziegfild Theatre and / casually ask for a carton of Gauloises and a carton / of Picayunes, and a NEW YORK POST with her face on it" (325). Even its epiphany is grounded in the urban quiddity of the POST headlines which remind him of "leaning on the john door in the 5 SPOT / while she whispered a song along the keyboard / to Mal Waldron and everyone and I stopped breathing" (324). This poem still explores a modernist sense of spatial and textual fragmentation: it shifts abruptly from the "casual" request for a carton of cigarettes to the Post's tragic headlines, it jumps arbitrarily from "12:20 in New York a Friday" to "three days after Bastille day" and back to a "shoeshine," and it ironically juxtaposes the dead singer's "whispered . . . song" with the live poet's "stopped breathing." It even invokes a quasi-poststructuralist inversion of absence over presence by eulogizing its exalted subject almost entirely in the margins of the text: not only does its lengthy detour through the poet's random urban wanderings repeatedly defer its narrative climax, but it also displaces the purportedly present subject of its eulogy onto the absent signifiers of the New York Post headlines and the poet's memories. There is a deliberate, complex modernist structure to the text, and yet that structure is infused with and heightened by a textual structure that closely follows the random and spontaneous topography of O'Hara's quotidian urban experiences. Consequently, the full meaning of the poem lies in its "ar(t)chitextural" synthesis of the complex aesthetic practices that it borrows from modernist art and its own textual experimentation with new literary strategies modeled after the dynamic rhythms of personal urban experiences. While the equilibrium between these interrelated dimensions of O'Hara's work frequently shifts, both abruptly and dramatically, toward either the urban or the artistic end of his poetic spectrum, many of O'Hara's most successful poems explore strikingly original interrelationships between the visual aesthetics of modern art and the socio-spatial topography of urban experience.

While "The Day Lady Died" combines diverse artistic and urban influences into a relatively stable synthesis, other O'Hara poems, such as

"Rhapsody," explore a more disjunctive amalgamation of visual and urban themes. On the one hand, "Rhapsody" explores the same abstract, eccentric, art-influenced kinds of spaces that we find in Guest's poetry, describing 515 Madison Avenue as a "door to heaven? portal / stopped realities and eternal licentiousness / or at least a jungle of impossible eagerness / your marble is bronze and your lianas elevator cables / swinging from the myth of ascending" (*Collected Poems*, 325–6). At the same time, however, this poem simultaneously describes the gritty urban experience of "getting into a cab at 9th Street and 1st Avenue / and the Negro driver tells me about a $120 apartment / 'where you can't walk across the floor after 10 at night / not even to pee, cause it keeps them awake downstairs'" (326). Yet, even though this poem explores a range of modernist and urban imagery in the same way that "The Day Lady Died" does, it refuses to synthesize these disparate images into any kind of stable aesthetic form. Instead, it deliberately juxtaposes disparate images in a seemingly random and disorderly manner, alternating between modernist and urban images without establishing any clear relationship between them. Even when it fuses them into hybrid images, these images are fraught with ambiguities and antagonisms instead of being synthesized into the kind of symbiotic hybrid form that we find in "The Day Lady Died." For example, the poem describes a "doorway linking 53rd with 54th / the east-bound with the west-bound traffic by 8,000,000s / o midtown tunnels and the tunnels, too, of Holland / where is the summit where all aims are clear" (326). This image makes gestures toward describing the spatial topography of New York City. It refers to specific streets, tunnels, and traffic directions, but it mixes these references up into a confusing modernist image that has no clear resolution. As the poem itself suggests, O'Hara's simultaneous engagement of modernist art and urban space produces a range of heterogeneous textual forms, some of which explore complex tensions and antagonisms between modern art and urban space. Instead of expressing some isomorphic correlation or developing some hybrid synthesis, the interrelated but unresolved modernist and urban images in this poem exist in an antagonistic relationship that produces no synthesis. They leave the reader wondering "where is the summit where all aims are clear / the pin-point light upon a fear of lust / as agony's needlework grows up around the unicorn / and fences him for milk- and yoghurt-work" (326). This kind of categorical confusion runs throughout O'Hara's work as it oscillates wildly between exploring the entire range of complex visual aesthetics practices that circulated among the post-WWII New York avant-garde and intricately mapping the socio-spatial topography of the city's heterogeneous urban spaces.

While these two artistic and urban dimensions of O'Hara's writing frequently cross paths, they rarely resolve themselves into any kind of coherent, stable, singular program. Instead, O'Hara's poems tend to engage some particular thematic or aesthetic interest briefly for a few lines, but then they quickly move on to engage some new issue or combination of issues. Like a juggler, O'Hara's poetry tends to keep several disparate interests suspended in an unresolved state of play without organizing them into any kind of stable structure. In this sense, O'Hara's dynamic aesthetic strategies are similar to both the complex visual aesthetics of de Konning's paintings and the ever-changing traffic on Second Avenue. Oscillating between modernist abstraction and an urban Pop vernacular, O'Hara's poetry not only resembles—but it also anticipated and influenced—the visual aesthetics of Second Generation New York school painters such as Jasper Johns, Grace Hartigan, and Robert Rauschenberg.

Nevertheless, the fundamental conceptual problem, the critical crux of my argument, remains unexplained. It is clear *that* O'Hara innovative aesthetic practices are strongly influenced by his passionate engagements with both the visual aesthetics of modernist art and the dynamic rhythms of complex heterogeneous urban spaces. As John Ashbery explains, O'Hara's poetry simultaneously explores "not only the space of New York School painting but of New York itself, that kaleidoscopic lumber-room where laws of time and space are altered" (x). But it is still not clear exactly *why* O'Hara and other post-WWII New York writers turned specifically to other artistic media outside the literary tradition in order to represent, analyze, and imagine alternatives to the spatial restructuring of post-WWII New York City? What is the relationship between the interart and urban dimensions of these writers' works, and why does O'Hara in particular insist that this relationship should remain disjunctive and constantly shifting?

As the post-WWII New York writer who most extensively explored both sides of this relationship between interart aesthetic experimentation and the complex socio-spatial topography of urban space, O'Hara's poetry provides important clues that can help us tentatively answer these kinds of questions. Even in an early poem like "Memorial Day 1950," O'Hara already begins exploring various interrelationships between modernist art and urban development by repeatedly juxtaposing images of modern artists and construction workers. He contrasts Picasso with his "axe going" against a "crew of creators" who "knocked down" in a "minute plane trees [. . .] outside my window" (*Collected Poems*, 17). He also describes the "Fathers of Dada" as carrying "shining erector sets" that "were lovely as chewing gum or flowers," and in almost direct response to Le Corbusier's maxim that buildings should be "machines for living in," he proclaims that "Poetry is as useful as a machine" because "naming things is only the intention / to make things" (17–8). Taken collectively, these images deconstruct post-WWII America's techno-rational, geometrical sense of architectural and urban construction. By ironically describing a "crew of creators" as "knock[ing] down" trees, O'Hara challenges the accuracy of our common sense notion of construction. His ironic word choices question whether a crew can be unproblematically described as "creators" if they have to "knock down" a previous order in order to create a new one. Similarly, his description of Picasso wielding an axe, as opposed to a paint brush, suggests that even artists perform creative acts that produce some kind of material effects. By describing Dada artists' "erector sets" as "lovely as chewing gum or flowers" and claiming that poetry is "as useful as a machine," he also suggests that there are other, more playful and less violent, kinds of construction. Moreover, his recurring associations between "Dada" and "erector sets" and between "poetry" and "machines" suggest that artistic creation does have materially significant consequences. Thus, O'Hara deconstructs post-WWII America's valorization of techno-rational architectural construction over the chaotic fragmentation of modernist aesthetic experimentation. Given that O'Hara considered Whitman, Crane, and Williams to be the only American poets "better than the movies," it is not surprising that he would turn to the more radical visual aesthetics of European modernist art and American abstract expressionist painting to find more appropriate models for the kind of complex, experimental aesthetic practices that he wanted to develop (*Collected Poems*, 498).

It is in O'Hara's more mature "I do this, I do that" and "lunch hour" poems, however, where we see most clearly why O'Hara and other post-WWII New York writers turned specifically to interart aesthetic practices in order to critically analyze the socio-spatial topography of post-WWII New York City. In poems such as "A Step Away from Them" and "Personal Poem," O'Hara describes his "lunch hour [. . .] walk among the hum-colored / cabs" and his "walk around a lunchtime" to "Moriarty's where I wait for / LeRoi [Jones]" (*Collected Poems*, 257, 335). While describing these "lunch hour" walks, each poem luxuriates in long detours through the seemingly meaningless quotidian minutiae of urban life. "A Step Away From Them" describes the ubiquitous construction workers feeding their "dirty / glistening torsos sandwiches / and Coca-Cola, with yellow helmets / on," the girls in skirts "flipping / above heels and blow[ing] up over / grates," and the "bargains in wristwatches" that O'Hara passes en route to Times Square (257). "Personal Poem" describes the "two charms" in O'Hara's pocket, the "construction to the left that closed the sidewalk," and the lady who "asks us for a nickel for a terrible / disease" (335). In the midst of these detailed accounts of the random scenes encountered during lunch hour walks to buy a cheeseburger at Juliet's Corner or to meet a friend at Moriarty's for some fish and ale, these poems insert recurring references to experimental artists and writers such as Jackson Pollock, Edwin Denby, Pierre Reverdy, LeRoi Jones, and Miles

Davis. By constantly oscillating between descriptions of quotidian urban experiences and references to experimental artists, these poems seem to suggest that there is some kind of relationship between the complex socio-spatial topography of post-WWII New York City and the complex aesthetic practices of modernist artists. They imply that the contingent, associative logic that connects the heterogeneous elements of urban life resembles the chaotic, fragmentary logic that structures modernist art. While O'Hara rejects any kind of simple, mechanical, one-to-one isomorphic correlation between these complex urban spaces and aesthetic practices, the more complex, subtle affinities that O'Hara explores between various kinds of aesthetic experimentation and particular urban spaces help explain why O'Hara and other post-WWII New York writers' turned so frequently to experimental interart aesthetic practices outside the literary tradition to represent and analyze the socio-spatial topography of urban space. For them, the postmodern turn in post-WWII American architecture and urbanism had already been prefigured in the fragmented aesthetics of modern and abstract expressionist art.

Conclusion

"Less is a bore"

Imagining The Postmodern City

LTIMATELY, THE NEW YORK AVANT-GARDE'S CRITIQUE OF POST-WWII AMERICAN urbanism contributed to the development of a new postmodern sense of space, or what Fredric Jameson describes as "postmodern hyperspace," a "new global space," or a "mutation in built space itself" (49, 44, 39). Advocating urban paradigms similar to those of the New York avant-garde, a new generation of postmodern architects and urbanists rose to prominence by challenging the fundamental premises of International Style Modernism. For example, Robert Venturi's *Complexity and Contradiction in Architecture* criticized modernism's "bland architecture," "blatant simplification[s]" and "puritanically moral language," while Colin Rowe and Fred Koetter's *Collage City* denounced modernism for its "sterile scientific rigour" and "lamentable lack of tolerance" (Venturi 22, 25; Rowe and Koetter 6, 132). Criticizing modernism's "dullness," "regimentation," "monotony, sterility and vulgarity," Jane Jacobs's *The Death and Life of Great American Cities* also attacked the "principles and aims that have shaped modern, orthodox city planning and rebuilding" (3–4, 7). From Team 10, the Independent Group, and COBRA to the Italian neorationalists, Situationists, and New Urbanists, a wide range of movements emerged in opposition to the central tenets of International Style Modernism.

While each of these movements criticized modernism for different reasons, the emerging postmodern consensus generally concurred that orthodox modernism constituted a fundamentally anti-urban project that undermined more than it promoted vibrant urban environments. Turning traditional urban planning on its head, Jacobs depicted modernism as an "unurban urbanization" that derived its basic principles from "towns, suburbs, tuberculosis sanatoria, fairs, and imaginary dream cities—from anything but cities themselves" (6–7):

This is not the rebuilding of cities. This is the sacking of cities. . . . In city after city, precisely the wrong areas, in light of planning theory, are decaying. Less noticed, but equally significant, in city after city the wrong areas, in light of planning theory, are refusing to decay. (4)

Like Ginsberg, Kaufman, and Joans, Jacobs argued that the techno-rational modernist city dehumanized and alienated urban subjects by creating "worse centers of delinquency, vandalism and general social hopelessness than the slums they were supposed to replace" (4). Like Sorrentino, Neal, and Touré, she criticized modernism for destabilizing urban communities, uprooting them "as if they were the subjects of a conquering power. . . . Whole communities are torn apart and sown to the winds" (5). Rather than conceptualizing cities as chaotic places that needed to be erased down to some kind of tabula rasa or ground zero and then reconstructed according to an abstract Cartesian geometry, Jacobs saw cities as places with a "most intricate and unique order" (447). The Situationists also described the "broad sweeps of the rationalist imagination, which had aspired to tailor the city with Cartesian precision" as a kind of anti-urban "butchery," while the Lettrist journal *Potlach* "dismissed le Corbusier as a 'cop' and nicknamed him Le Corbusier-Sing-Sing after the notorious prison" because he "aspire[d] to *suppress the street*" (Sadler 20, 50). Like the post-WWII New York avant-garde, the emerging postmodern movement repeatedly attacked modernism for attempting to deny, suppress, police, and destroy the complex, heterogeneous topography of urban spaces. Postmodern critics saw modernism as an all-out assault on everything urban, including the spatial topography of urban environments, the social psychology of urban subjects, the political economy of urban communities, and the aesthetics and politics of urban cultures.

To counter this antiurban ideology, postmodern architects and urbanists began advocating more complex spatial practices that encouraged greater urban diversity. Parodying the Miesian maxim, "less is more," with his own postmodern counterclaim that "[l]ess is a bore," Venturi called for a new architecture of "complexity and contradiction," while Rowe and Koetter promoted a more "open" and "critical" urbanism that would embrace the "most disparate stimuli, hostile to neither utopia nor tradition, while by no means value free the city as museum discloses no intimations of urgent belief in the value of any all-validating principle" (Venturi 21–22, 25; Rowe and Koetter 132). Jacobs also defended the value of "dense" urban spaces with a "fantastically dynamic" kind of "organized complexity" rooted in a "most intricate and close-grained diversity of uses" (14, 16). Within this emerging postmodern consensus there was no shortage of alternative proposals for how to reconstruct more complex and heterogeneous kinds of urban spaces: Guy Debord's unitary urbanism, Peter Smithson's cluster city, Rowe and Koetter's collage city, Aldo van Eyck's

cities of "labyrinthine clarity," Constant Nieuwenhuys's New Babylon, and
Reyner Banham's eclectic manifesto, "City as Scrambled Egg," all
advanced alternative postmodern urban paradigms. Rejecting modernism's
"twin fantasies of order and omnipotence," Rem Koolhaas even challenged
urban planners to embrace a "Nietzschean frivolity" that takes "insane
risks," dares to be "utterly uncritical," and fundamentally reconceptualizes
urban planning as the:

> staging of uncertainty; it will no longer be concerned with the arrangement of
> more or less permanent objects but with the irrigation of territories with poten-
> tial; it will no longer aim for stable configurations but for the creation of enabling
> fields that accommodate processes that refuse to be crystallized into definitive
> form; it will no longer be about meticulous definition, the imposition of limits, but
> about expanding notions, denying boundaries, not about separating and identify-
> ing entities, but about discovering unnameable hybrids; it will no longer be
> obsessed with the city but with the manipulation of infrastructure for endless
> intensifications and diversifications, shortcuts and redistributions—the reinvention
> of psychological space. (*S, M, L, XL,* 969)

It is precisely this anti-modernist reconceptualization of space as "open,"
"complex," "hybrid," "labyrinthine," and "uncertain" that postmodernism and the post-WWII New York avant-garde share in common, and
both movements have made this a central tenet of their urban visions.

Recognizing this strong family resemblance, it is tempting to describe
the post-WWII New York avant-garde as simply an early manifestation of
some kind of proto-postmodernism, and there is certainly some truth to
such a characterization. The avant-garde's alternative spatial sensibilities
did help shape the emerging postmodern consensus, but there are also significant and irreducible differences between the avant-garde's utopian
urbanism and contemporary postmodernism. Postmodern spaces such as
the New Times Square, Trump Tower, and Philip Johnson's AT & T
Building do reject modernist sobriety, but they do not really realize the
urban visions of Ellison, Ferlinghetti, and O'Hara—let alone Ginsberg,
Kaufman, and Scott-Heron. In fact, many postmodern spaces oppose more
than they achieve the utopian urbanism advocated by the post-WWII New
York avant-garde. Whatever gains postmodernism has made in complicating architectural forms, challenging modernist taboos against ornamentation, and promoting ludic alternatives to modernist sobriety, it has generally continued and at times even extended modernism's anti-urbanism.
Instead of promoting real urban diversity, postmodern urbanization often
subjugates cities to purely commercial purposes, playing no small role in
what the *Harvard Design School Guide to Shopping* describes as shopping's colonization of "almost every aspect of urban life":

Town centers, suburbs, streets, and now airports, train stations, museums, hospitals, schools, the Internet, and the military are shaped by the mechanisms and spaces of shopping. The voracity by which shopping pursues the public has, in effect, made it one of the principal—if only—modes by which we experience the city. . . . Perhaps the beginning of the twenty-first century will be remembered as the point where the urban could no longer be understood without shopping. (Harvard Project on the City 1)

Even when postmodern spaces such as Charles Moore's Piazza d'Italia or Baltimore's Harbor Place attempt to celebrate urban diversity, they do so largely in a superficial manner that tends to reduce Venturi's architectural complexity to a mere "architecture of spectacle" that "draw[s] a veil over real geography through construction of images and reconstructions, costume dramas, staged ethnic festivals, etc." (Harvey 87, 91). Instead of complicating and diversifying cities, postmodernism often creates mere "fantasy world[s]" of decontextualized historical references and cultural simulacra that extend "beyond current realities into pure imagination" (Harvey 97). In his trenchant critique of postmodern Los Angeles, Mike Davis goes so far as to define the "real *Zeitgeist* of postmodernism" as precisely its "profoundly anti-urban impulse, inspired by unfettered financial forces and a Haussmannian logic of social control" (113). Far from providing the antidote to modernism's "unurban urbanization," postmodern urbanism seems to have reinfected American cities with a more virulent strain of modernism's anti-urban virus. More modernist than post, contemporary architecture and urbanism have rejected modernist sobriety by redressing American cities in more colorful and complicated facades, but postmodernism's failure to effectively remedy modernist anti-urbanism still hangs around its neck like an albatross. Postmodernists have successfully promoted Venturi's decorated sheds and ludic theme-space shopping malls, but there has been little progress in realizing Jacobs's sense of the city as "organized complexity," let alone the "Nietzschean frivolity" and "staging of uncertainty" advocated by Koolhaas.

Consequently, even though postmodernism and the post-WWII New York avant-garde share many common goals, these two movements have ultimately evolved along divergent paths—with Ginsberg's "negro streets at dawn" and Kaufman's "jazz corners" veering off toward the political activism and urban riots of the late 1960s, while postmodern urbanization has largely promoted the revaunchist gentrification, commercial populism, and alienated bunker architecture of the 1980s. As Mary McLeoad has noted, "many leftist architects and critics" characterize postmodernism's "pseudohistorical nostalgia," "fabricated traditions," "pandering to a nouveau-riche clientele," and "abandonment of any social vision" as an "architecture of Reaganism" (McLeod 680). It seems much more difficult, however, to reduce Ginsberg's "Howl," O'Hara's "The Day Lady Died," and Kaufman's "Abomunist Manifesto" to some corollary "culture of Reaganism." Despite its theoretical defense of complex, heterogeneous urban spaces, postmodernism has largely failed to achieve the utopian urbanism advocated by the New York avant-garde or even by postmodern theorists themselves, and this failure seriously complicates any simplistic comparisons between these two movements. In fact, characterizing the post-WWII New York avant-garde simply as a precursor to the postmodern actually inverts its real relationship to postmodernism. The avant-garde not only proposed a more radical and progressive urban vision than has been realized by most postmodern architects and urbanists, but its spatial sensibility was fundamentally grounded in a radically pro-urban defense of complex, heterogeneous urban spaces, which postmodern urbanism has at least significantly diluted—if not altogether abandoned and betrayed. Even if the avant-garde did not produce an ideologically pure revolutionary art, its imaginative explorations of urban space did envisage something bolder than such classic postmodern spaces as the Las Vegas Strip, the New Times Square, and John Portman's Westin Bonaventure Hotel or Renaissance Center. If a comparison is to be drawn between the post-WWII New York avant-garde and postmodernism, it seems more accurate to describe post-modernism as a watered-down version of—if not an anti-urban and depoliticized betrayal of—the avant-garde's utopian ideals. To reduce the New York avant-garde to merely a postmodern precursor is to miss what is most significant about it. Far from being a prelude to the future, the New York avant-garde imagined utopian urban possibilities that still remain largely unrealized. From O'Hara and Kaufman to Ginsberg and Baraka, post-WWII New York writers, artists, and intellectuals advocated various kinds of postmodern spatial practices that resemble the largely unrealized theories of Jacobs, Koolhaas, and Constant more than the Venturi-esque architecture and New Urbanist communities that now dominate America's new postmodern landscape.

But what exactly has caused this divergence, and what are its aesthetic and political consequences? The simplest way to explain how the avant-garde's utopian urbanism devolved—rather than evolved—into the contemporary postmodern city is to note that postmodern spatial theories have only been partially and selectively realized, usually in ways that co-opt postmodernism's more radical possibilities to the pragmatic realities of powerful economic and political interests. Postmodern architects and urbanists have advocated a wide range of spatial theories, ranging from Venturi's populist commercialism, Frank Ghery's architectural irony, and Daniel Libeskind's deconstructive fragmentation to Aldo Rossi's urban artifacts, Jacobs's multi-use urban neighborhoods, and the ludic Situationist designs of Constant's New Babylon. All these architects and urbanists reject the rigid sobriety of International Style Modernism, but their different critiques of modernism also advance diverse—sometimes complimentary and other times conflicting—postmodern alternatives. Robert Venturi, Denise Scott Brown, and Steve Izenour might concur with Jacobs that we should learn from "existing landscape[s]" and analyze "how cities work in real life," but their turn toward Las Vegas's "skyline of signs" and "architecture of urban sprawl" produces very different results than Jacobs's interest in the "organized complexity" of "dense" urban spaces such as Greenwich Village (Venturi, Scott Brown, and Izenour 3; Jacobs 4, 14, 16). Both Las Vegas and Greenwich Village offer excellent counter-examples to modernism, but they challenge modernism in different ways and for different historical and political purposes. By following Venturi's sense of postmodern space more closely than Jacobs's, the postmodern redevelopment of American cities has shifted more away from than toward the utopian urbanism of the post-WWII New York avant-garde. Even when movements such as New Urbanism have invoked Jacobs's theories, they have tended to simplify and adapt them to suburban contexts—such as Seaside, Florida or the Disney Corporation's Celebration—which are spatially, socially, and culturally removed from the "dense" urban contexts advocated by Jacobs. Recognizing the diversity of these conflicting postmodern theories and practices, McLeod characterizes postmodernism as a "complex matrix" that includes "instances of both social entrenchment and genuine critique," and she suggests that postmodernism has generally degenerated from "being essentially a movement that criticized aesthetic and social parameters to one that affirms the status quo" (686, 689). As McLeod's description demonstrates, postmodern urbanism has not simply continued or extended the post-WWII New York avant-garde's utopian urbanism, but rather it has produced a complex amalgamation of postmodernisms that mixes the avant-garde's utopianism with more conservative socio-spatial practices. If we are to appreciate fully the aesthetic and political significance of the avant-garde's urban vision, it is crucial that we recognize how it both resembles and differs from the postmodern movements that have followed after it. We must also draw more precise analogies between the New York avant-garde and specific kinds of postmodernism to better illuminate both the similarities and the differences between distinct postmodern strategies. For example, it is more useful to compare O'Hara's "lunch hour" poems with the Situationists' psychogeographical research methods than it is to compare Ginsberg's critique of the corporate city in "Howl" with the populist commercialism of *Learning from Las Vegas*. Similarly, Kaufman's representations of urban space share more in common with Mike Davis's and Edward Soja's geopolitical analyses of urban space than they do with Lynch's notion of cognitive mapping. The ultimate goal of my own analysis, therefore, is less to propose some grand theory about the relationship between the post-WWII New York avant-garde and some particular theory of postmodernism than it is to suggest that these two movements share a complex range of finely-nuanced interrelationships that are sometimes congruent, sometimes complimentary, and sometimes diametrically opposed.

Without idealizing the avant-garde as an ideologically pure cultural revolution, I do believe that its critical explorations of urban space can help us better understand not only how postmodern urbanism has evolved/devolved, but also how it could have developed—and perhaps even still can develop—along different paths. Even though the avant-garde advocated a very postmodern spatial sensibility, it was more adept at steering clear of the aesthetic and political collusions that have transformed postmodernism into "*the* new corporate style" with an "amazing rapidity" (McLeod 685). In particular, I would argue that the New York avant-garde retained its progressive critical edge by fusing its postmodern defense of dense, complex, heterogeneous urban spaces with a strong geopolitical critique of how the capitalist political economy powerfully shapes the historical evolution of urban spaces. Instead of simply advocating a formalist sense of spatial complexity-for-complexity's-sake, the avant-garde promoted a more complex sense of urban space as a socio-spatial continuum where spatial, cultural, and political forces interact. They did advocate an alternative utopian urbanism, but they remained highly suspicious of corporate capitalism's power to dominate, control, and police even the most counter-hegemonic urban spaces. Even in the midst of Ginsberg's, Kaufman's, and Baraka's most radical explorations of urban diversity, there are constant reminders that the powerful corporate city of Moloch—with its high stakes real estate investments, towering corporate skyscrapers, and heavily armed police forces—constantly threatens and menaces the city. In this sense, the avant-garde's understanding of urban space shares a lot in common with the geopolitical urban analyses developed by the Situationists, the Marxist architectural historian Manfredo Tafuri, World-Cities theorists, and neo-Marxist urban sociologists and geographers such as Henri Lefebvre, David Harvey, Edward Soja, and Mike Davis. It also has more affinities with the deconstructive theories of Bernard Tschumi, Mark Wigley, and Daniel Libeskind—who look more critically at the difficulties of constructing truly revolutionary spatial practices—than it does with the more celebratory and formalistic postmodern theories advanced by Venturi, Jencks, and Lynch.

Unlike the avant-garde, however, postmodern architecture and urbanism have often failed to combine these two formal and political dimensions. As Mary McLeod explains, one of postmodernism's "most positive social impact[s]" has been its "rejection of the modern movement's urban vision," but it has often failed to synthesize its critique of modernism with a critical analysis of its own "relation to the powers at large" (689).

Venturi's simplistic promotion of Las Vegas's populist commercial architecture, Joel Garreau's boosterist promotion of edge cities as new hybrid urban-surbaban frontiers, and the postmodernization—i.e. commercialization, gentrification, and Disneyification—of the New Times Square represent only some of the most obvious examples of this failure to critically analyze cities in their geopolitical contexts, but a similar undertheorization of corporate capitalism's impact upon postmodern architecture and urbanism extends in different ways throughout the work of many postmodernists and New Urbanists. By refocusing attention back on the post-WWII New York avant-garde's utopian urbanism, I hope to encourage us to analyze spatial theories and practices more critically both by connecting postmodern spaces to their geopolitical contexts and by making us more aware of the historical evolution of American spatial practices. By gaining a greater awareness of the historical precedents that have caused our cities to become what they now are, I believe that we can become better critics and better citizens of those cities in which we live—and we can also learn to make more responsible choices about the future cities that our society will some day construct.

Most importantly, I have attempted to provide glimpses of utopian possibilities that have only been incompletely and fleetingly glimpsed in the history of American urbanism. For me, the real value of the avant-garde's explorations of urban space derives precisely from its still largely unrealized utopian vision. Unlike the 1939–40 New York World's Fair which produced an urban model that was more-or-less faithfully followed by post-WWII American urbanists, the avant-garde's utopian urbanism has only exerted a minor influence on the historical evolution of postmodern architecture and urbanism. As explorers and defenders of post-WWII New York City's marginal spaces, the cultural avant-garde became chroniclers of cities lost and urban spaces less traveled, and their accounts of those marginal urban spaces can still inspire us today to think more deliberately and more boldly about the cultural and political significance of urban spaces.

Bibliography

Abu-Lughod, Janet. *New York, Chicago, Los Angeles: America's Global Cities*. Minneapolis: University of Minnesota Press, 1999.

Altieri, Charles. *Enlarging the Temple: New Directions in American Poetry During the 1960s*. Lewisburg, PA: Bucknell University Press, 1979.

Appadurai, Arjun. *Modernity at Large: Cultural Dimensions of Globalization*. Minneapolis: University of Minnesota Press, 1996.

Ashbery, John. Introduction to *The Collected Poems of Frank O'Hara*, edited by Donald Allen. Berkeley: University of California Press, 1995.

Ashanti, Baron James. "Just Another Gig." In *The Second Set: The Jazz Poetry Anthology, Volume 2*, edited by Sascha Feinstein and Yusef Komunyakaa. 4–5.

Bachelard, Gaston. *The Poetics of Space*. Translated by Maria Jolas. Boston: Beacon Press, 1964.

Baldwin, James. "Fifth Avenue, Uptown." *Esquire*, July 1960, 70–73, 76.

Baraka, Amiri. "AM/TRAK." In *The Jazz Poetry Anthology*, edited by Sascha Feinstein and Yusef Komunyakaa. 2–7.

———. *The Autobiography of LeRoi Jones/Amiri Baraka*. New York: Freundlich, 1984.

Belgrad, Daniel. *The Culture of Spontaneity: Improvisation and the Arts in Postwar America*. Chicago: University of Chicago Press, 1998.

Beller, Miles. *Dream of Venus (Or Living Pictures): A Novel of the 1939 New York World's Fair*. Beverly Hills: C. M. Publishing, 2000.

Binder, Eando. "Rope Trick." *Astounding Science Fiction*, April 1939, 74–88.

Bowers, Neal. "The City Limits." In *Frank O'Hara: To Be True to a City*, edited by Jim Elledge. Ann Arbor: University of Michigan Press, 1990.

Breslin, James E. B. *From Modern to Contemporary: American Poetry, 1945–1965*. Chicago: University of Chicago Press, 1984.

Brooks, Gwendolyn. *In the Mecca*. New York: Harper & Row, 1968.

Brown, Arthur. "The Assassination of Charlie Parker" In *The Second Set: The Jazz Poetry Anthology, Volume 2*, edited by Sascha Feinstein and Yusef Komunyakaa. 20–21.

Buddensieg, Tilmann. Introduction to *Nietzsche and "An Architecture of Our Minds,"* edited by Alexandre Kostka and Irving Wohlfarth. Los Angeles: Getty Research Institute for the History of Art and the Humanities, 1999.

Cusker, Joseph P. "The World of Tomorrow: Science, Culture, and Community at the New York World's Fair." In *Dawn of a New Day: The New York World's Fair 1939/40*, edited by Helen Harrison. New York: New York University Press, 1980.

Davis, Mike. "Urban Renaissance and the Spirit of Postmodernism." *New Left Review* 151 (1985): 106–13.

De Legall, Walter. "Psalm for Sonny Rollins." In *Understanding the New Black Poetry: Black Speech and Black Music as Poetic References*, edited by Stephen Henderson. 202–3.

Demas, Corinne. *Eleven Stories High: Growing Up in Stuyvesant Town, 1948–1968*. Albany: State University of New York Press, 2000.

Derrida, Jacques. *Writing and Difference*. Translated by Alan Bass. Chicago: University of Chicago Press, 1978.

di Donato, Pietro. *Christ in Concrete*. New York: Signet, 1993.

Doctorow, E. L. *World's Fair*. New York: Plume, 1985.

Eliot, T. S. *The Waste Land and Other Poems*. New York: Signet, 1998.

Ellison, Ralph. *Invisible Man*. 2d ed. New York: Vintage, 1995.

Fainstein, Norman I., Susan S. Fainstein, and Alex Schwartz. "Economy Shifts and Land Use in the Global City: New York, 1940–1987." In *Atop the Urban Hierarchy*, edited by Robert A. Beauregard. Totowa, NJ: Rowman & Littlefield, 1989.

Feinstein, Sascha and Yusef Komunyakaa, eds. *The Jazz Poetry Anthology*. Bloomington: Indiana University Press, 1991.

Feinstein, Sascha and Yusef Komunyakaa, eds. The *Second Set: The Jazz Poetry Anthology, Volume 2*. Bloomington: Indiana University Press, 1996.

Ferlinghetti, Lawrence. *A Coney Island of the Mind*. New York: New Directions, 1974.

———. "Modern Poetry is Prose" In *Literature and the Urban Experience: Essays on the City and Literature*, edited by Michael C. Jaye and Ann Chalmers Watts. New Brunswick: Rutgers University Press, 1982.

———. "Poetry and City Culture." Poet Laureate of San Francisco Inaugural Speech. 13 October 1998. <http://www.citylights.com/poetlaureate.html> (8 March 2003).

Fiedler, Leslie. *The Collected Essays of Leslie Fiedler*, vol. 2. New York: Stein and Day, 1971.

Fitzgerald, F. Scott. *The Great Gatsby*. New York: Simon & Schuster, 1995.

Foucault, Michel. *The Order of Things: An Archaeology of the Human Sciences*. New York: Vintage, 1973.

———. "Of Other Spaces." Translated by Jay Miskowiec. *Diacritics* 16.1 (1986): 22–27.

Franklin, H. Bruce. "America as Science Fiction: 1939." In *Coordinates: Placing Science Fiction and Fantasy*, edited by George E. Slusser, Eric S. Rabkin, and Robert Scholes. Carbondale, IL: Southern Illinois University Press, 1983.

Fraser, Kathleen. "One Hundred and Three Chapters of Little Times: Collapsed and Transfigured Moments in the Fiction of Barbara Guest." In *Breaking the Sequence: Women's Experimental Fiction*, edited by Ellen G. Friedman and Miriam Fuchs. Princeton: Princeton University Press, 1989.

Geddes, Norman Bel. *Magic Motorways*. New York: Random House, 1940.

Gelernter, David. *1939, The Lost World of the Fair*. New York: Avon Books, 1995.

General Motors Corporation. *Futurama*. New York: General Motors Corporation, 1940.

Giedion, Sigfried. *Space, Time, and Architecture: The Growth of A New Tradition*. Cambridge: Harvard University Press, 1980.

Ginsberg, Allen. *Collected Poems, 1947–1980*. New York: Harper & Row, 1984.

Greenberg, Clement. "The Crisis of the Easel Picture." *Partisan Review* 15.4 (1948): 481–84.

———. "The Decline of Cubism." *Partisan Review* 15.3 (1948): 366–69.

Groening, Matt. *Futurama #1*. Los Angeles: Bongo Comics, 2000.

Guest, Barbara. *The Blue Stairs*. New York: Corinth, 1968.

———. *Poems: The Location of Thing, Archaics, The Open Skies.* New York: Doubleday, 1962.

———. "A Reason for Poetics." *Ironwood* 24 (Fall 1984): 153–55.

———. *Seeking Air.* Los Angeles: Sun & Moon Press, 1997.

———. *Selected Poems.* Los Angeles: Sun & Moon Press, 1995.

Harvard Project on the City. *Harvard Design School Guide to Shopping.* Köln: Taschen, 2001.

Harvey, David. *The Condition of Postmodernity: An Enquiry into the Origins of Cultural Change.* Cambridge, MA: Blackwell, 1990.

Henderson, David. *De Mayor of Harlem.* New York: E. P. Dutton, 1970.

Henderson, Stephen. *Understanding the New Black Poetry: Black Speech and Black Music as Poetic References.* New York: William Morrow, 1973.

Hillman, Barbara. "The Artful Dare: Barbara Guest's *Selected Poems.*" *Talisman: A Journal of Contemporary Poetry and Poetics* 16.1 (1996): 207–20.

Hitchcock, Henry-Russell and Phillip Johnson. *The International Style.* New York: W. W. Norton, 1966.

Holmes, John Clellon. *Go.* New York: Scribners, 1952.

Howe, Irving. "Mass Society and Post-Modern Fiction." *Partisan Review* 26 (1959): 420–36.

———. "The New York Intellectuals." In *Selected Writings, 1950–1990.* New York: Harcourt Brace Jovanovich, 1990. 240–80.

Hull, Lynda. "Orinthology." In *The Second Set: The Jazz Poetry Anthology, Volume 2,* edited by Sascha Feinstein and Yusef Komunyakaa. 87–9.

Jacobs, Jane. *The Death and Life of Great American Cities.* New York: Vintage, 1961.

James, Henry. *The American Scene,* edited by John F. Sears. New York: Penguin, 1994.

Jameson, Fredric. *Postmodernism, or, The Logic of Late Capitalism.* Durham: Duke University Press, 1991.

Joans, Ted. *A Black Manifesto in Jazz Poetry and Prose.* London: Calder and Boyars, 1971.

———. *All of Ted Joans and No More.* New York: Excelsior, 1961.

Kaufman, Bob. *Cranial Guitar: Selected Poems.* Minneapolis: Coffee House Press, 1996.

———. "Battle Report." In *The Jazz Poetry Anthology,* edited by Sascha Feinstein and Yusef Komunyakaa. 110.

Kerner Commission. *Report of the National Advisory Commission on Civil Disorders*. New York: Bantam, 1968.

Kerouac, Jack. *On the Road*. New York: Penguin, 1991.

Kofsky, Frank. *John Coltrane and the Jazz Revolution of the 1960s*. New York: Pathfinder, 1998.

Koolhaas, Rem. *Delirious New York: A Retroactive Manifesto for Manhattan*. New York: Monacelli, 1994.

———. *S, M, L, XL*. New York: Monacelli, 1996.

Le Corbusier. *The City of To-morrow and its Planning*. Translated by Frederick Etchells. New York: Payson & Clarke, 1929.

Lefebvre, Henri. *The Production of Space*. Trans. Donald Nicholson-Smith. Cambridge, MA: Blackwell, 1991.

Lhamon, W. T. *Deliberate Speed: The Origins of a Cultural Style in the American 1950s*. Washington, D. C.: Smithsonian Institution Press, 1990.

"Life Goes to the Futurama." *Life*, June 5, 1939, 79–85.

Lopate, Phillip, ed. *Writing New York: A Literary Anthology*. New York: The Library of America, 1998.

Mailer, Norman. "Mailer vs. Scully." *The Big Bite*, May 1963, 37–40.

Manousos, Anthony. "Barbara Guest." *Dictionary of Literary Biography: American Poets Since World War II*, vol. 5., edited by Donald J. Greiner. Detroit: Gale, 1980. 295–300.

McLeod, Mary. "Architecture and Politics in the Reagan Era: From Postmodernism to Deconstructivism." In *Architecture Theory Since 1968*, edited by K. Michael Hayes. Cambridge, MA: MIT Press, 1998.

Meikle, Jeffrey L. *Twentieth Century Limited: Industrial Design in America, 1925–1939*. Philadelphia: Temple University Press, 1979.

Melville, Herman. *Bartleby and Benito Cereno*. New York: Dover, 1990.

Micheline, Jack. *North of Manhattan: Collected Poems, Ballads, and Songs, 1954–1975*. San Francisco: Manroot, 1976.

Mitchell, W. J. T. *Picture Theory: Essays on Verbal and Visual Representation*. Chicago: University of Chicago Press, 1994.

Moses, Robert. "Indefinable New York." *Esquire*, July 1960, 52.

Myers, John Bernard. *The Poets of the New York School*. New York: Gotham Book Mart, 1969.

Neal, Larry. "Don't Say Goodbye to the Pork-Pie Hat." In *The Second Set: The Jazz Poetry Anthology, Volume 2*, edited by Sascha Feinstein and Yusef Komunyakaa. 143–46.

Nielsen, Aldon Lynn. *Black Chant: Languages of African-American Postmodernism*. New York: Cambridge University Press, 1997.

Nye, David. *Narratives and Spaces*. New York: Columbia University Press, 1998.

Official Guide Book. New York: Exposition Publications, 1939.

O'Hara, Frank. *The Collected Poems of Frank O'Hara*, edited by Donald Allen. Berkeley: University of California Press, 1995.

———. *Poems Retrieved*, edited by Donald Allen. Revised edition. San Francisco: Grey Fox Press, 1996.

Oppen, George. *Collected Poems*. New York: New Directions, 1975.

Perloff, Marjorie. *The Dance of the Intellect: Studies in Poetry of the Pound Tradition*. New York: Cambridge University Press, 1985.

———. *Frank O'Hara: Poet Among Painters*. New York: George Braziller, 1997.

Prodhoretz, Norman. "The Know-Nothing Bohemians." *Partisan Review* 25.2 (1958): 305–18.

Pynchon, Thomas. *Gravity's Rainbow*. New York: Penguin, 1973.

Reynolds, Malvina. "Little Boxes." *Ear to the Ground*. Washington, D.C.: Smithsonian Folkways, 2000.

Rodgers, Carolyn. *Songs of a Blackbird*. Chicago: Third World, 1969.

Rowe, Colin and Fred Koetter. *Collage City*. Cambridge, MA: MIT Press, 1978.

Sadler, Simon. *The Situationist City*. Cambridge, MA: MIT Press, 1998.

Sanchez, Sonia. *We A BaddDDD People*. Detroit: Broadside Press, 1970.

Schwartz, Delmore. "The Present State of Poetry." In *Selected Essays of Delmore Schwartz*, edited by Donald A. Dike & David H. Zucker. Chicago: University of Chicago Press, 1970.

Scott, William B. and Peter M. Rutkoff. *New York Modern: The Arts and the City*. Baltimore: Johns Hopkins University Press, 1999.

Scott-Heron, Gil. *Small Talk at 125th and Lenox: A Collection of Black Poems*. New York: World Publishing Company, 1970.

Scully, Vincent. "Mailer vs. Scully." *The Big Bite*, May 1963, 37–40.

Sorrentino, Gilbert. *Steelwork*. New York: Dalkey Archive Press, 1992.

Stern, Robert A. M., Gregory Gilmartin, and Thomas Mellins. *New York 1930: Architecture and Urbanism Between the Two World Wars*. New York: St. Martin's, 1995.

———. *New York 1960: Architecture and Urbanism Between the Second World War and the Bicentennial*. New York: Monacelli Press, 1995.

Stevens, Wallace. *The Collected Poems of Wallace Stevens*. New York: Vintage, 1990.

Stone, Le Roy. "Flamenco Sketches." In *Understanding the New Black Poetry: Black Speech and Black Music as Poetic References*, edited by Stephen Henderson. 194–95.

Susman, Warren. *Culture as History*. New York: Pantheon, 1984.

Telotte, J. P. *A Distant Technology: Science Fiction Film and the Machine Age*. Hanover, NH: Wesleyan University Press, 1999.

Thomas, Lorenzo. "Ascension: Music and the Black Arts Movement." In *Jazz Among the Discourses*, edited by Krin Gabbard. Durham: Duke University Press, 1995. 256–74.

Touré, Askia Muhammad. "Extension." In *Understanding the New Black Poetry: Black Speech and Black Music as Poetic References*, edited by Stephen Henderson. 304–06.

———. Touré, Askia M. *From the Pyramids to the Projects: Poems of Genocide and Resistance!*. Trenton: Africa World Press, 1990.

———. "JuJu." In *The Second Set: The Jazz Poetry Anthology, Volume 2*, edited by Sascha Feinstein and Yusef Komunyakaa. 171–74.

Troupe, Quincy. *Skulls Along the River*. New York: Reed & Cannon Co., 1984.

Venturi, Robert. *Complexity and Contradiction in Architecture*. New York: Museum of Modern Art, 1966.

Venturi, Robert, Denise Scott Brown, and Steven Izenour. *Learning from Las Vegas*. Revised edition. Cambridge, MA: MIT Press, 1977.

Virilio, Paul. "The Overexposed City." In *Rethinking Architecture: A Reader in Cultural Theory*, edited by Neil Leach. New York: Routledge, 1997.

Wallock, Leonard. "Introduction" and "New York City: Capital of the Twentieth Century." In *New York: Cultural Capital of the World, 1940–1965*, edited by Leonard Wallock and William Sharpe. New York: Rizzoli, 1988.

White, E. B. "They Come Home with Joyous Song." *New Yorker*, May 13, 1939, 25–28.

Whyte, William H., Jr. *The Organization Man*. New York: Simon & Schuster. 1956.

Wolfe, Tom. *From Bauhaus to Our House*. New York: Washington Square Press, 1981.

Womack, Jack. *Terraplane: A Futuristic Novel of New York, 1939*. New York: Tom Doherty Associates, 1988.

Index